AF608996

Marc Mimram
Airtime

Marc Mimram

Structure | Light · Landscapes of Gravity · Airtime

Through the Lens of Erieta Attali

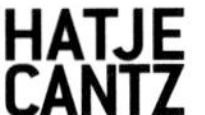

Construction site of the Airtime Building, May 2017

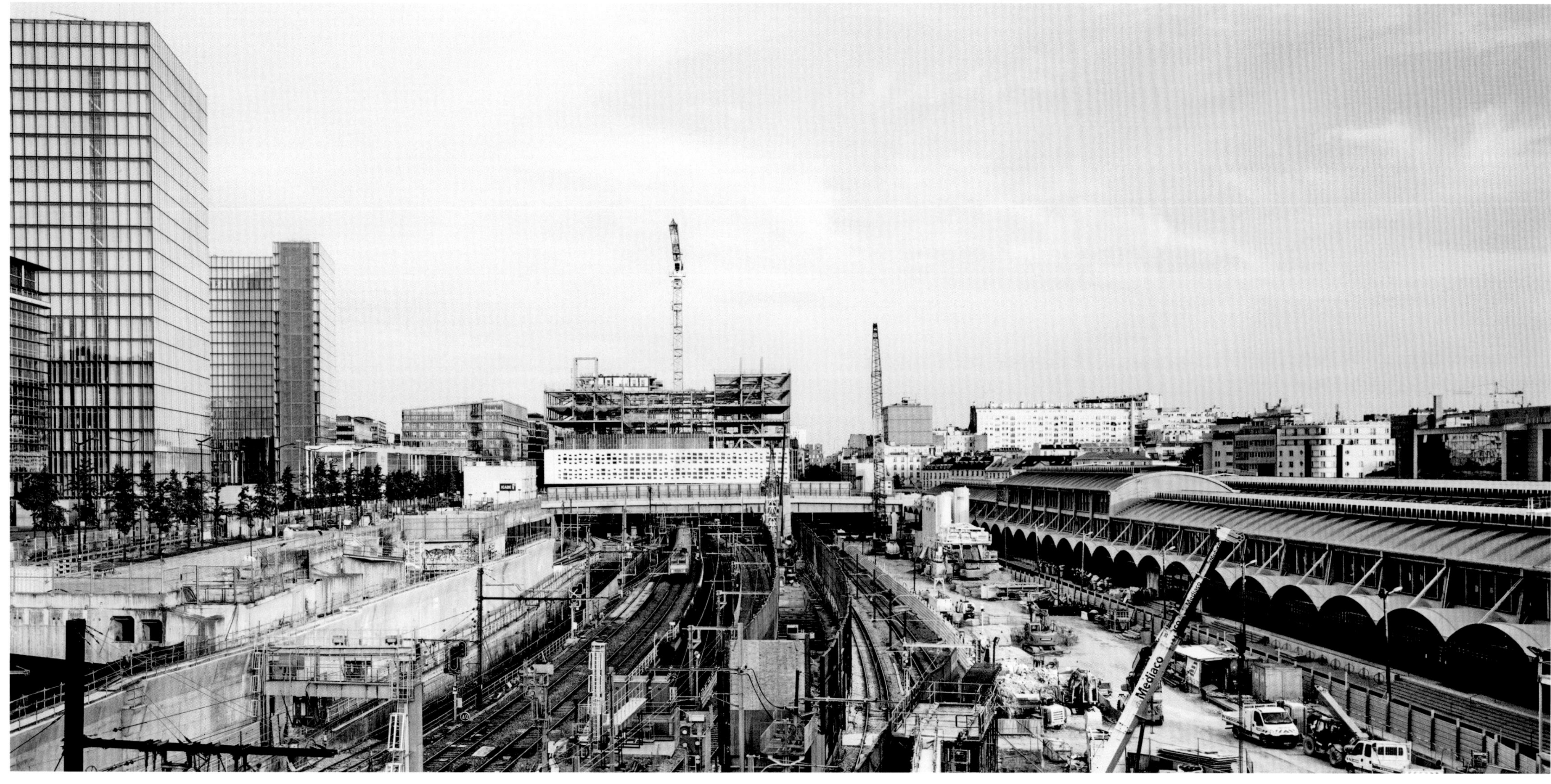

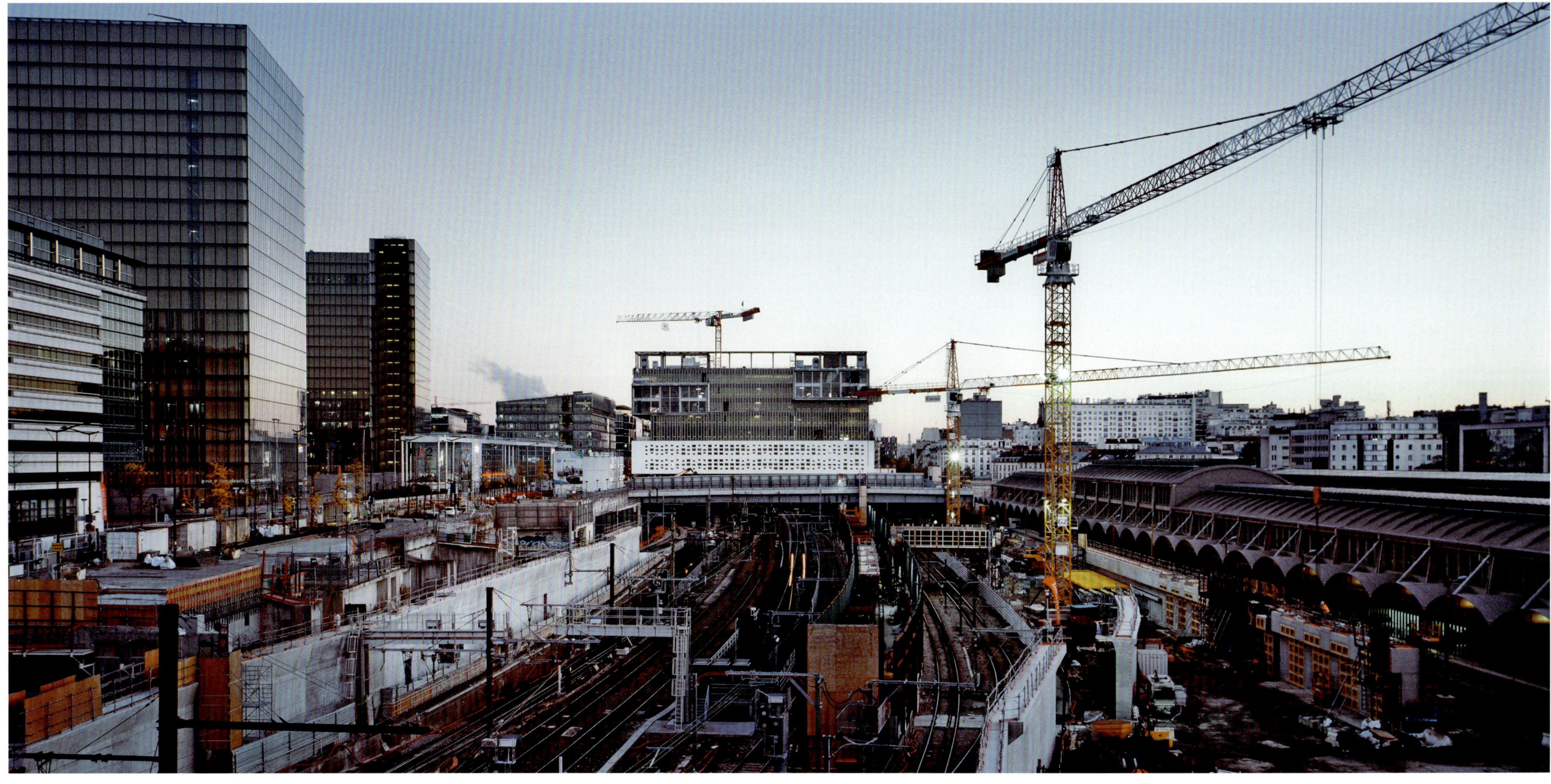

November 2018

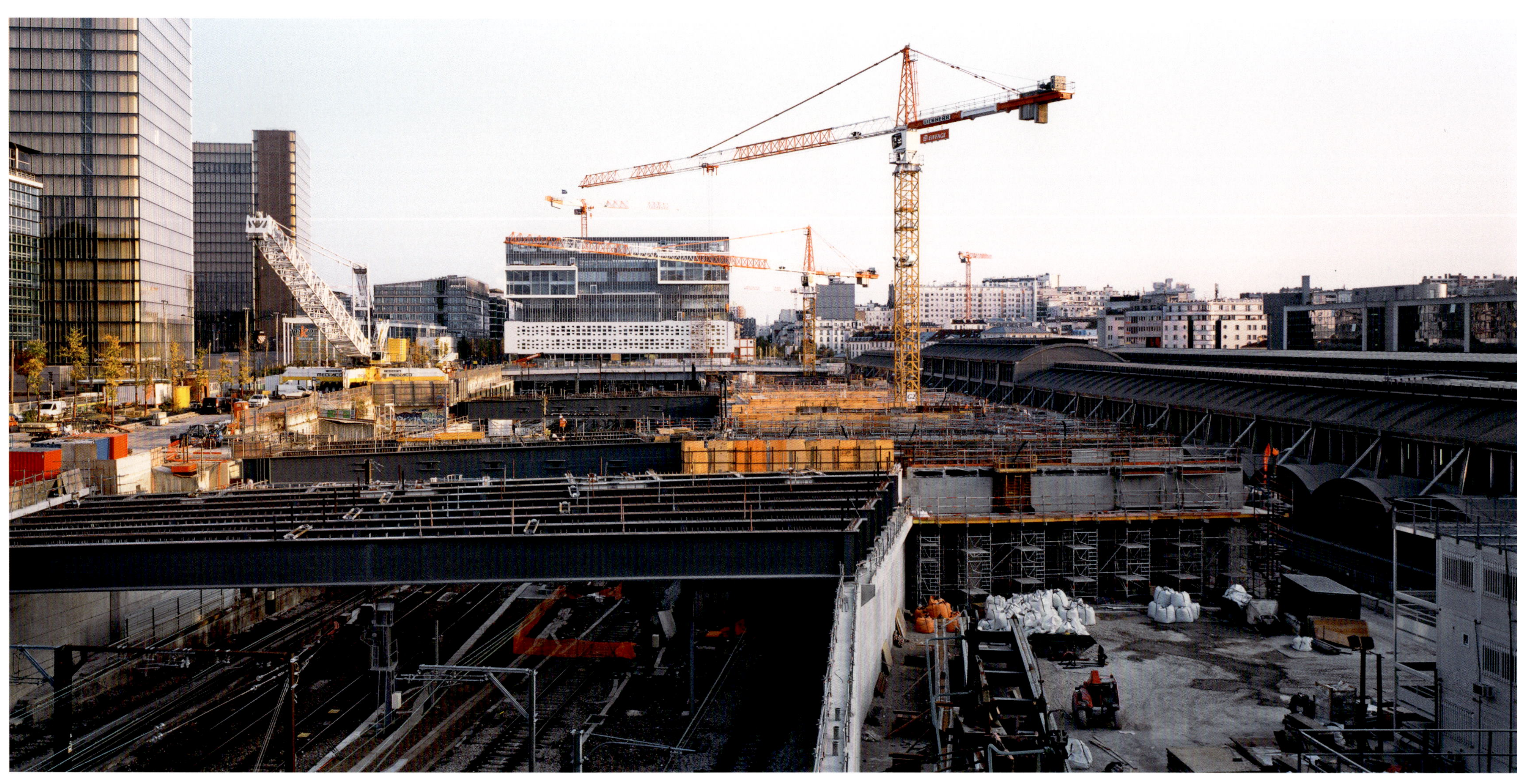

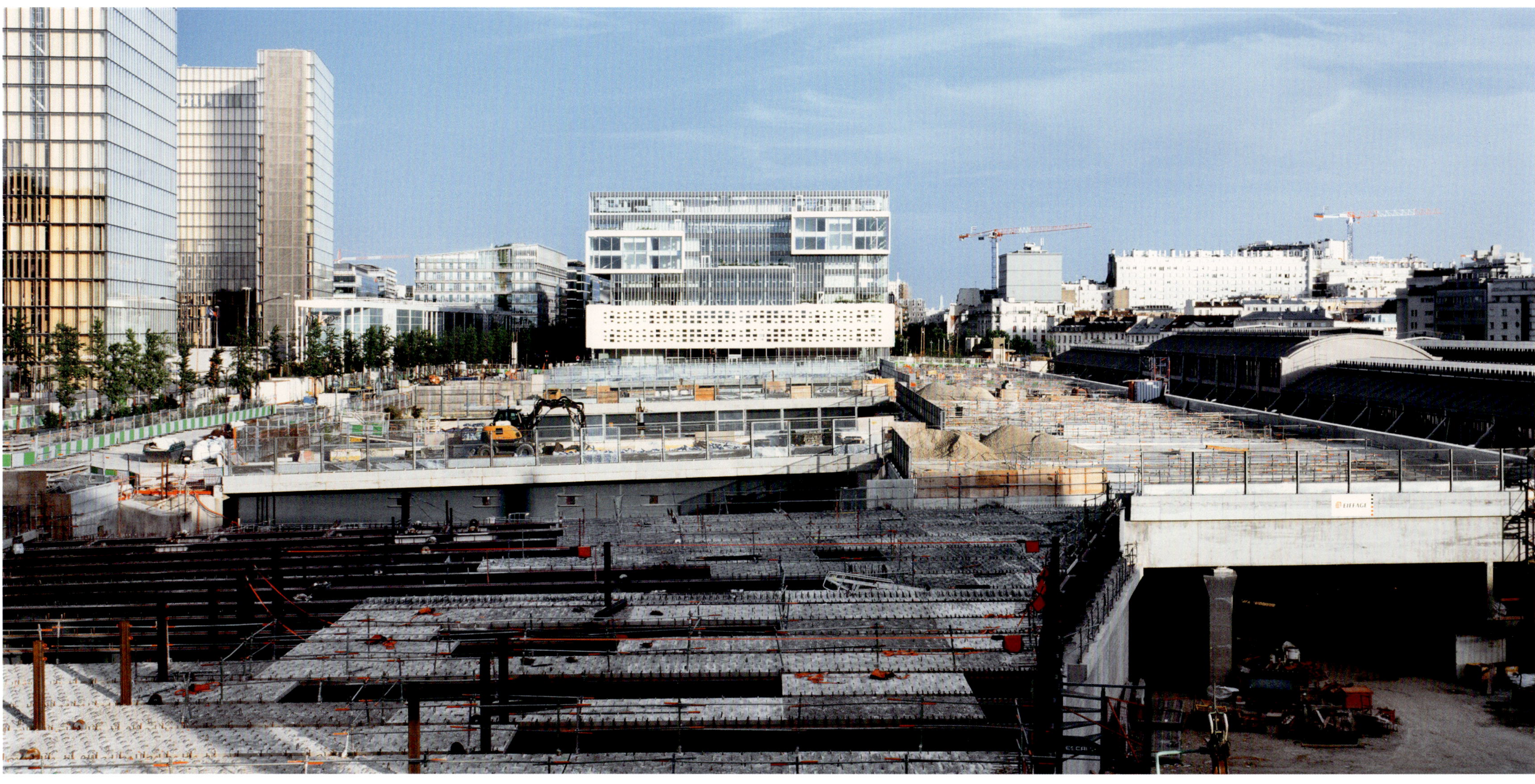

Airtime Building
Marc Mimram

Flowing like a river between the Avenue de France and Halle Freyssinet are the railway lines, now wider, now merging together. Here, to the right of the Airtime Building, the possible area without intermediate supports is 58 meters (190 feet). Everywhere else, the buildings being erected over the railway network have been constructed on a thick platform, a table of concrete on which any collection of buildings conforming to the rules of urban development can be erected at random without planning ahead of time. Urban planners have abandoned the idea of the *tabula rasa* in favor of a *tabula nova*: a platform waiting to be developed. This approach is irrational and wasteful. Furthermore, it cannot be transposed to the right of the project because the span is too great, intermediate supports only being possible if a costly reconstruction of the rail infrastructure were to be undertaken.
Our proposal approaches the problem from the other end. Instead of installing an initial platform, we have suggested suspending the platform forming the roof over the rails from the bridging building. This new theory changes the economic equation, allowing the cost of the invisible platform structure to be integrated with that of the superstructure of the building, this particular geographical arrangement allowing for a different kind of architecture.

As designed, the building thus becomes a bridge-building resting on either side of the tracks, which are 58 meters apart, its 16,000 tons being suspended above the trains. The effect of this structural arrangement is liberating, making it possible to make particular use of gravitational stresses. Since the stresses are concentrated in the floors forming the bridging structure, the other parts of the building are free. Suspended from or resting on the main structure, they can vary in thickness and embrace elements such as terraces, balconies, loggias, or mezzanines—all different ways of expanding the working space depending on orientations and views.
This choice of structural design makes it possible to develop comfortable tertiary spaces. The different areas and spaces extending from the office areas open onto the city or are screened from it by the use of corbelling. The working areas are able to enjoy these extensions, whether shared or individually acquired. Paradoxically, these very generous arrangements are the result of the structural constraints of the bridge design and the resolution of the problem of the railway lines by integrating the roof over the tracks into the design rather than using an inefficient supporting platform that would only increase the overall cost of the project.
The architecture gains in coherence, and the structure itself is implied without drawing attention to itself. Tomorrow, the railway lines below will disappear along with the whole network beneath the new construction, but the extraordinary method used will continue to evoke their presence. The beams of the main bridging are concentrated in the floors with façades pierced with a pattern recalling the Vierendeel beams used. The terraces included on the suspended or supported floors are freely varied. Both the memory of the fabrication process and that of the work site are embodied in an architecture that does not necessarily flaunt its muscles but which reveals itself without camouflage, without concealing its initial determining geographical condition. The project sprang from this coherent view; its realization becomes architecture.

Regaining the Urban Horizon

The tertiary project developed between the Bibliothèque de France and Halle Freyssinet crosses the railway lines. This is not to say, however, that it should ignore the urban landscape to which it belongs—quite the opposite. In our view, the bridge formed by the project anchors it in its surroundings in the 13th arrondissement, a magnificent geographical and constructed topography extending from the towers of Porte d'Italie on the horizon towards Butte aux Cailles, between the Gobelins and La Salpêtrière, and, in the distance, Ivry and Gentilly. All these places can be seen exceptionally well from the building, entering into a dialogue with it and establishing its architecture: in exchange, we offer this panorama.
The project occupies a very specific place in the development of the Paris Rive Gauche area, and particularly along the Avenue de France. To the northeast it looks over the towers of the Bibliothèque de France, towards the Parc de Bercy, on an axis with the footbridge over the Seine. This link is particularly significant because it marks a slope in the ground here and anchors the new Rive Gauche over the roads of the 13th arrondissement of the past.
Taking the constraints of the bridge-like structure as a starting point, the project aims to create new conditions of use of a tertiary building. It is the intention to enter into a dialogue with the city in relation to these new conditions of use.
Our structural and morphological research has been guided by these considerations. The project seeks to take advantage of its exceptional structure—more work of art than building—in order to generate in turn exceptional situations. The structure

required to bridge the railway lines gives great freedom of form to the envelope and, given the specific opportunities of the site and the views it offers, allows it to include places of use directed at the surrounding urban landscape: continuous balconies, double height spaces, terraces, and framed views.

The Environment as a Condition of Use

We would like to see dialogue with the city as a central feature of the development of the project. The situation of being able to see out is echoed by the possibility of being seen. The building standing here is not just in alignment with others, it is also part of a remarkable perspective. The city, the horizon, the sky, and also lights and orientations are all environmental conditions, and we want these to guide the new tertiary uses put forward by the project.

The specific situation of a bridge-building makes it possible to create structures separate from the spanning elements—the great bridging beams spanning 58 meters—which are simultaneously suspended over the floors below and resting on them. Thanks to the difference of these elements from the larger structures, terraces, double height spaces, and loggias can be inserted between the structural elements.

Tertiary occupation can move away from its geometrical logic (1.35 meters (4.4 feet) long by 18 meters (59 feet) wide, with an unlit central section) to discover new dimensions, varying from 6 to 19 meters (19.6 to 62.3 feet) wide, dual aspect offices, and free levels with different façades or external extensions.

It is our aim to reconsider the requirements and take advantage of the freedom offered by structures such as this to create new conditions of work in the tertiary sector. The world of offices has become too rule bound. Here we have an opportunity to innovate, offering a variety of new, adaptable, and differentiated ways of working. Moving away from the traditional style of office, here we can create work places that open out on to the city, extended by shared spaces, horizontal spaces for socializing such as the covered terraces, or vertical balconies in the form of mezzanines. Our project opens the way and encourages new styles of working in the tertiary sector, promoting conviviality in the workplace and putting in place arrangements that bring people together under the best possible conditions.

The building makes use of the constraints imposed by its bridging structure to create variations in usage. The environmental quality here is derived from the different uses, orientations, and openings on to the city horizon. The project develops and takes shape in line with the possibilities offered by the structure for its orientation in the urban landscape.

Stabilized Equilibrium

The need to design a structure to bridge the railway tracks below might have resulted in a compact, massive building, anchored by previously constructed supports, but we decided on a different approach. We make use of gravity, with its ability to create sophisticated groupings, constructing a framework of ribs rising from ground level, suggesting a "stabilized equilibrium."

The load-bearing elements are of two types, with those bridging the railway below being different from those used for the transversal portals. While all the load-bearing elements are indivisibly linked, they nevertheless appear to be separate from one another. They are brought together in the heart of the building at the newel of the stairs that has the function of transferring the vertical load.

The idea was essentially to make a suspended building. The bridging structure was not simply the result of the need to span a wide area; it was also a liberating element where the directions of the protruding main beams offer multiple aspects and arrangements. Apparently disconnected, the large beams are assembled to provide portals and structural compositions, stabilized around the central newels, the structural load being taken up by two supports installed on Avenue de France and along the tree-lined walkway to the south.

We were not aiming for an extreme form of structural expressionism. We sought rather to make use of the strength of the bridging elements necessary to the project.

The structure here serves the dialogue between urban life and usage. It is the structure that liberates the panorama and that brings about a variety of usages.

The suspended mass of these large structural elements leads us to think about gravitational forces, but in a way that is more sensitive to the pleasures of the place and more generous in respect to the pleasure to be taken from being there.

The treatment of the façade is inspired by the duality of elements that support and elements that are supported. The bridging elements reveal the constraints imposed on them in a single and massive envelope pierced in a rhythm echoing the curves of the forces that run through the façade beam. The suspended or balanced parts that are fitted in between the weight-bearing volumes are an expression of an absence of constraints. Their extreme lightness is expressed in a glass skin or a simple, single curtain wall. The contrast between these two types of envelope places the weight-bearing elements in a situation of suspension.
The supports represent an important aspect of the project. They are geometrically predefined as to position and size. In order to avoid making them the most important feature of a project more concerned with its relationship to the city and the need to adapt to the scale of the passerby, the supports are integrated into an arrangement that, on the large scale, evokes a stabilized equilibrium and, locally, combines load transfer with a simple geometric form.
The skill is visible but is not omnipresent. The order in which the building can be read sets it within the scale of the city.

A Shared Building Site

The work is finished. The nights when the bridging structures were thrown across the railway lines have passed slowly with the rhythm of a work of art. The *crash deck* formed by the platform over the lines is now suspended from the main beams. The large bridging structures concentrate the gravitational load onto 58 meters of supports (two on Avenue de France and four on the tree-lined walkway) dispersed between 199 compression spring boxes introduced to suppress vibration from the trains below. The building's 16,000 tons are gently shared between the spring boxes.
The structure is alive, it changes shape, recovers its counter-jib and changes again according to its varying occupations. A few centimeters towards the top, up to 12 centimeters (4.7 inches) at the bottom. It doesn't seem much: the structure is rigid.
Rigidity and flexibility: even the façades are suspended in order to allow for this random and controlled movement. The building does not shake and seems oblivious to the passing trains.
The offices open on to long terraces that extend the working areas in all directions over the city, near and far: benches, plants, and electric sockets will open up the office spaces, too often isolated from the rest of life, making them more homely and more empathetic.
Looking out from the corbelled windows, over the river, between the towers of the Bibliothèque de France, in the distance to Notre-Dame and the Eiffel Tower and nearer at hand to the tower blocks of the 13th arrondissement, the new working spaces seem very different from offices that have for so long conformed to a standard pattern.
This building is not standard, nor should life at work be standard. You search in vain for a reception desk: there is no central spot, no one to guide you, no management to manage. No typical floors, but the prospect of openness, complexity informed by orientation, views, depths, varying occupations according to ways of living in the workplace.
In the transparency of the inner courtyard, the suspended spaces float above a garden, the trains passing invisibly below.

Memories of Construction

Memory of the passing trains,
Memory of the men working on the spiderweb-like framework,
Memory of the work and knowledge accumulated through the process of construction, transformed into protection, ordered into architecture.

Architecture comes out of the material of the world metamorphosed into a way of thinking about spaces in which to live. The resistance of materials governs structure.
The mental images reside in the memory, that of the pleasures of creating in the uncompromising world of the building site. Architecture is this mental projection, that of our designs metamorphosed into ordered nature, balanced structure, built space. The images of the project provide the evidence; we wanted to share them through the grainy surface of photographs taken with a film camera as they progressed from hidden to visible, from raw state to completion.
A shared memory; a unique story.

March 2017

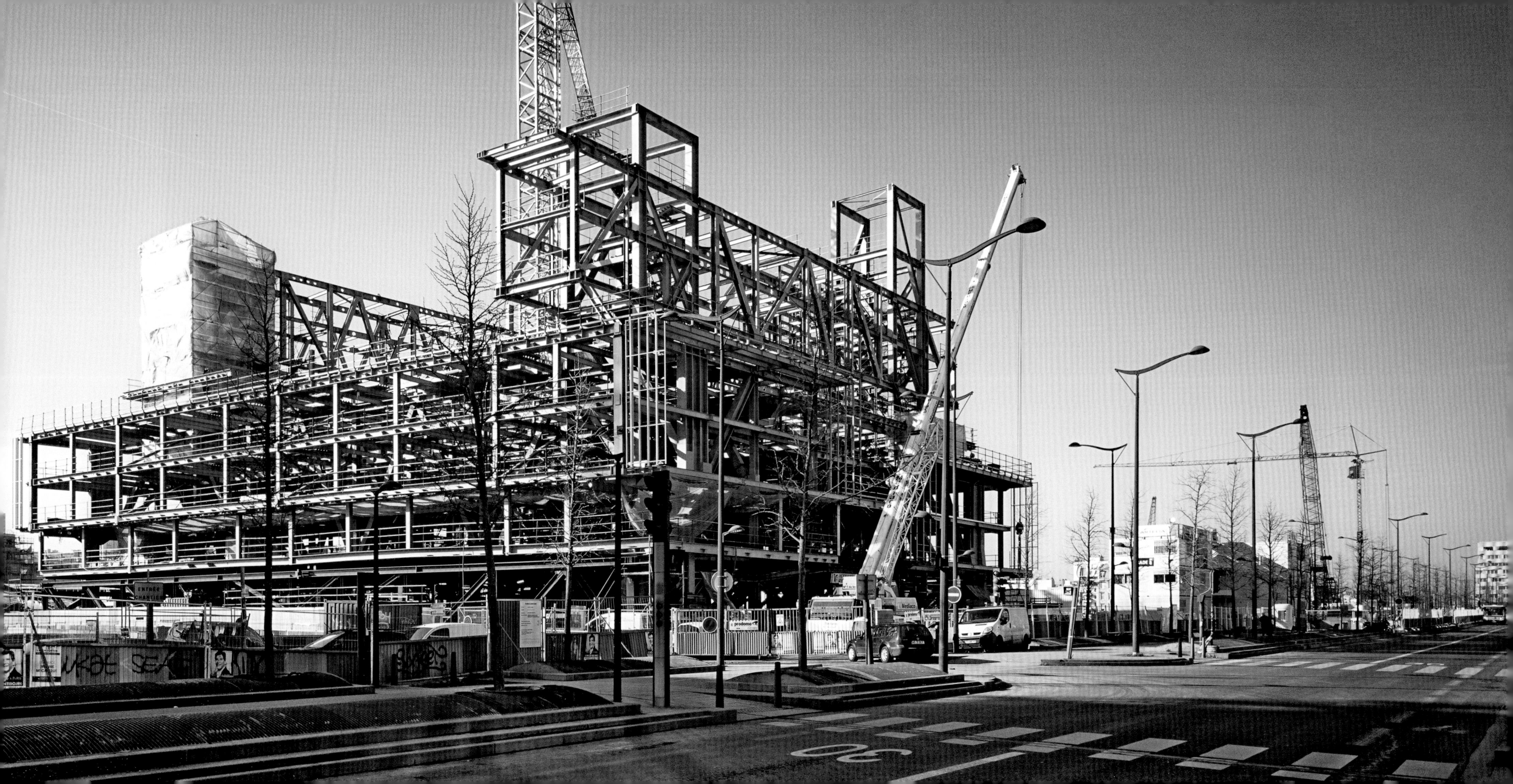
ENTRÉE
CHANTIER
prodomo
Mediaco

March 2017

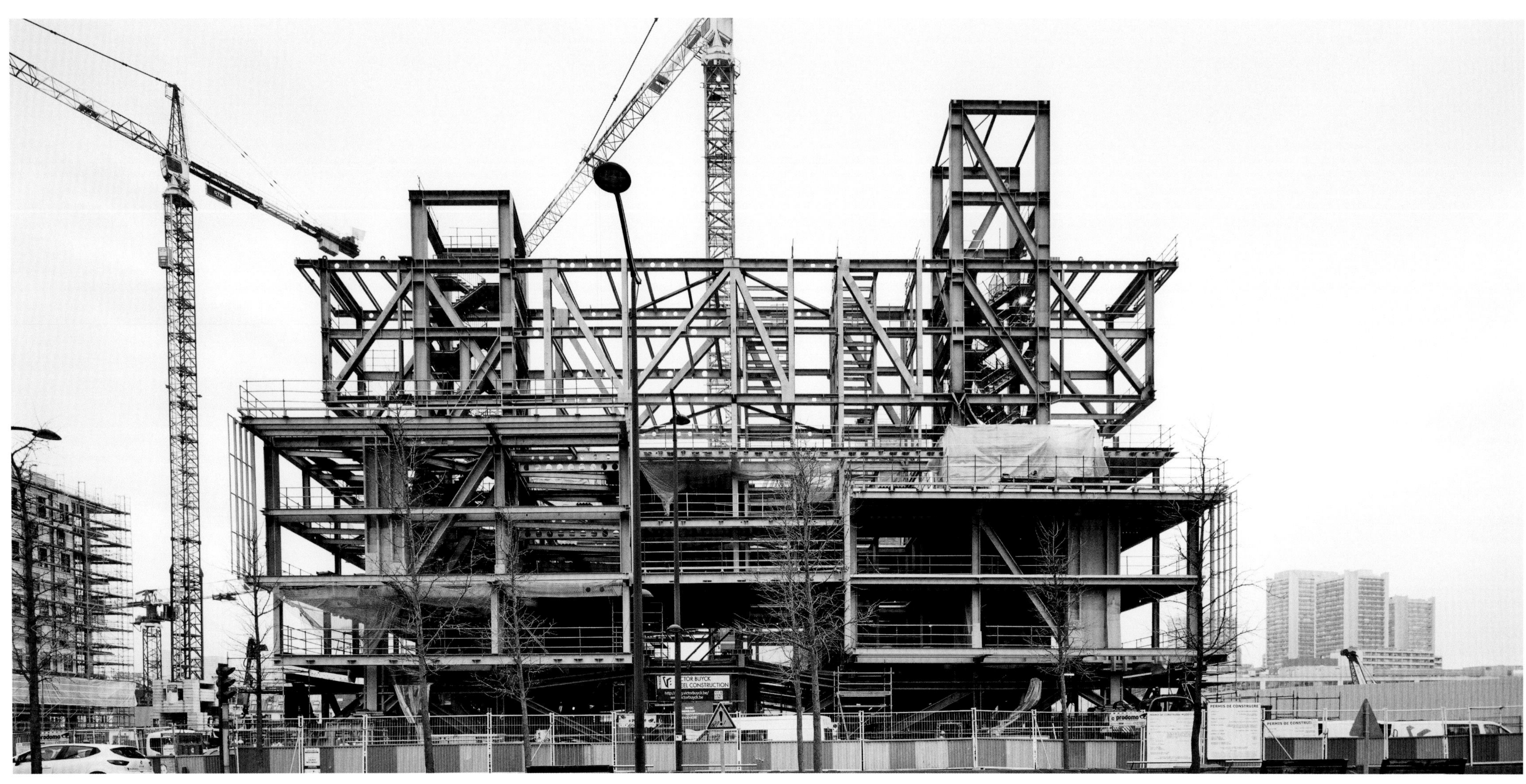

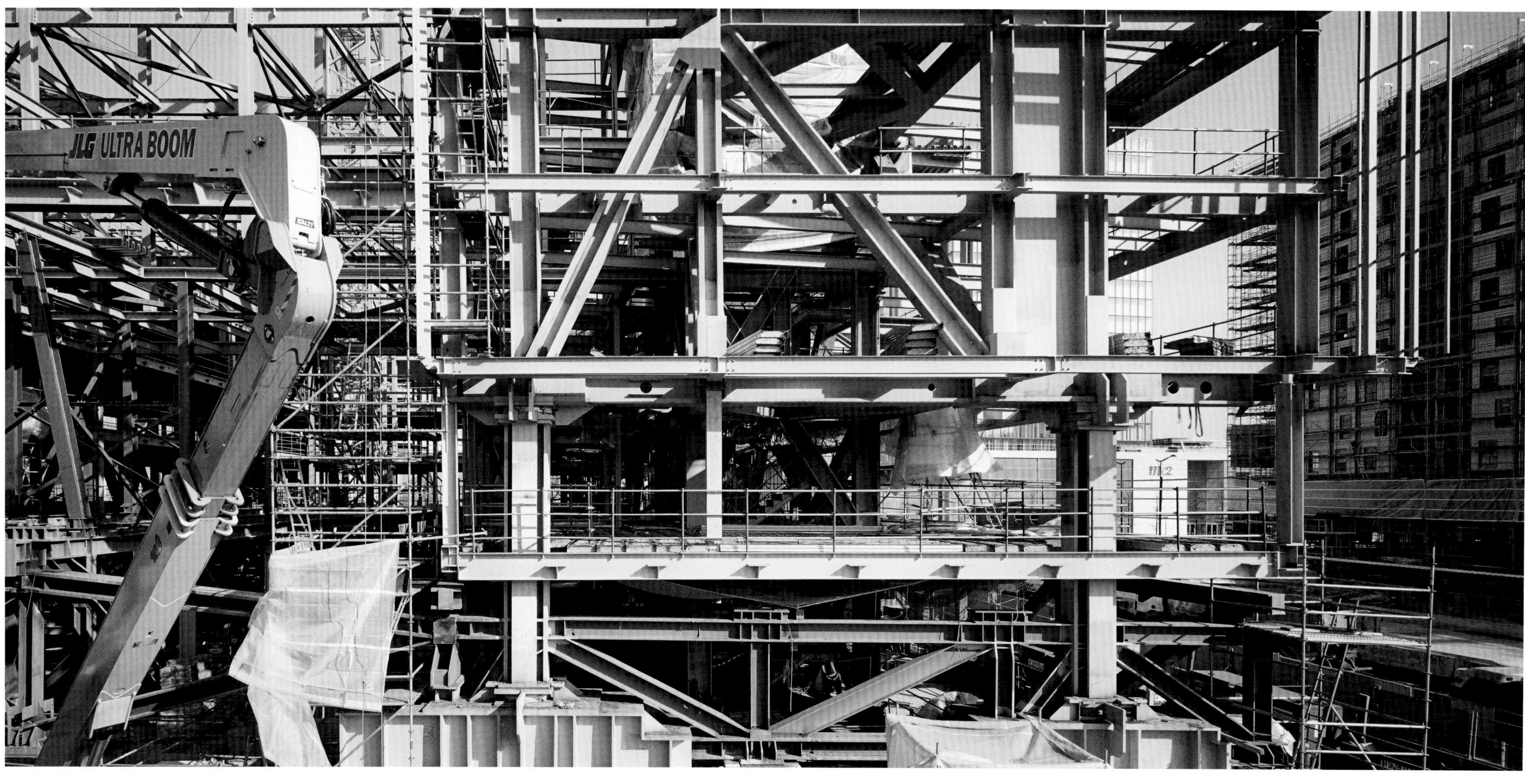
JLG ULTRA BOOM

March 2017

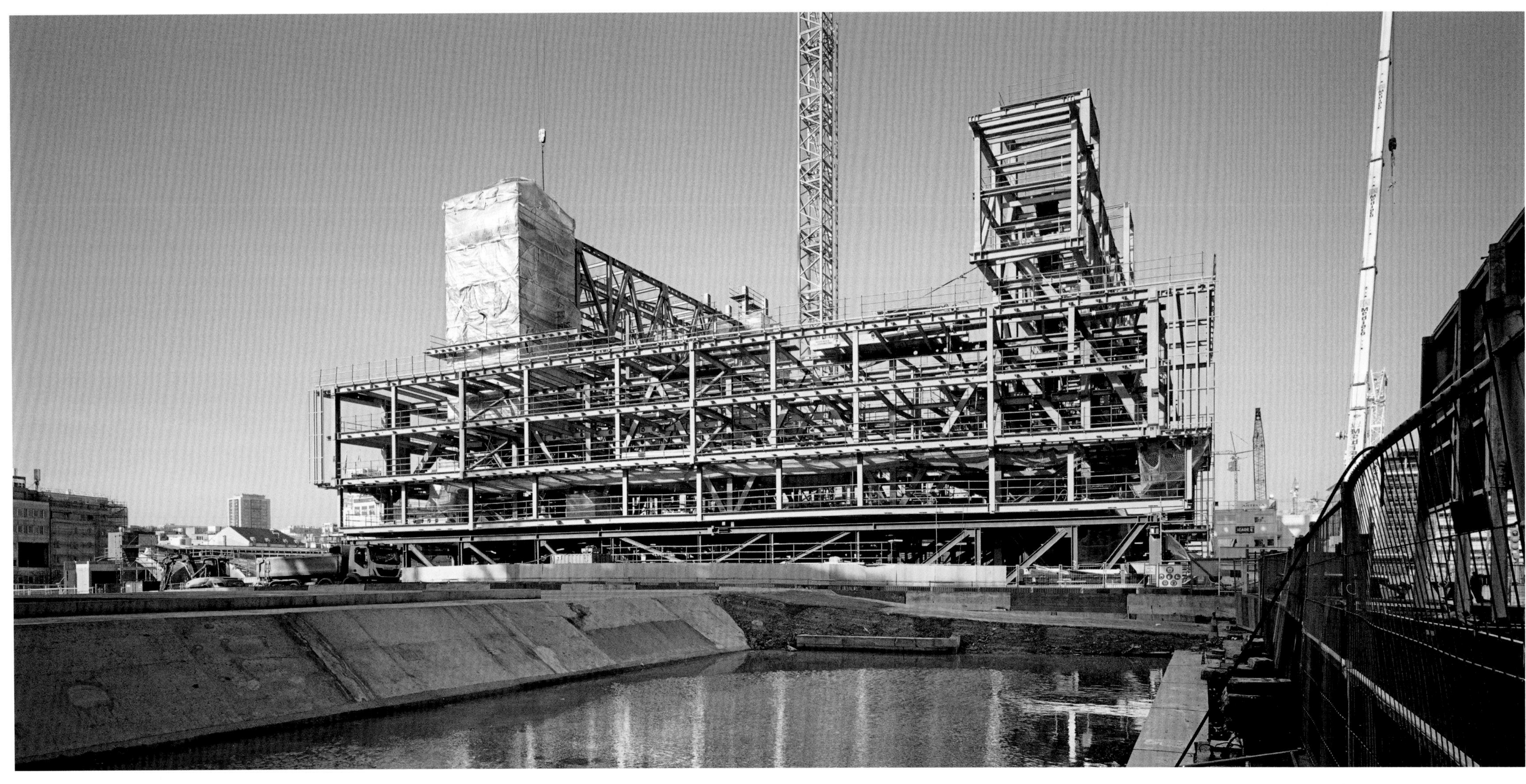

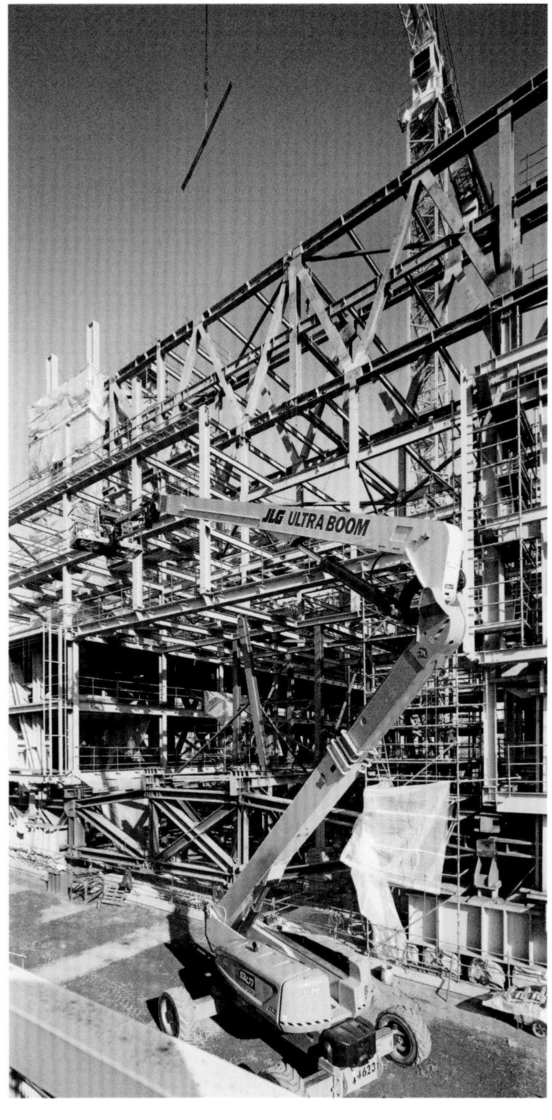
JLG ULTRA BOOM

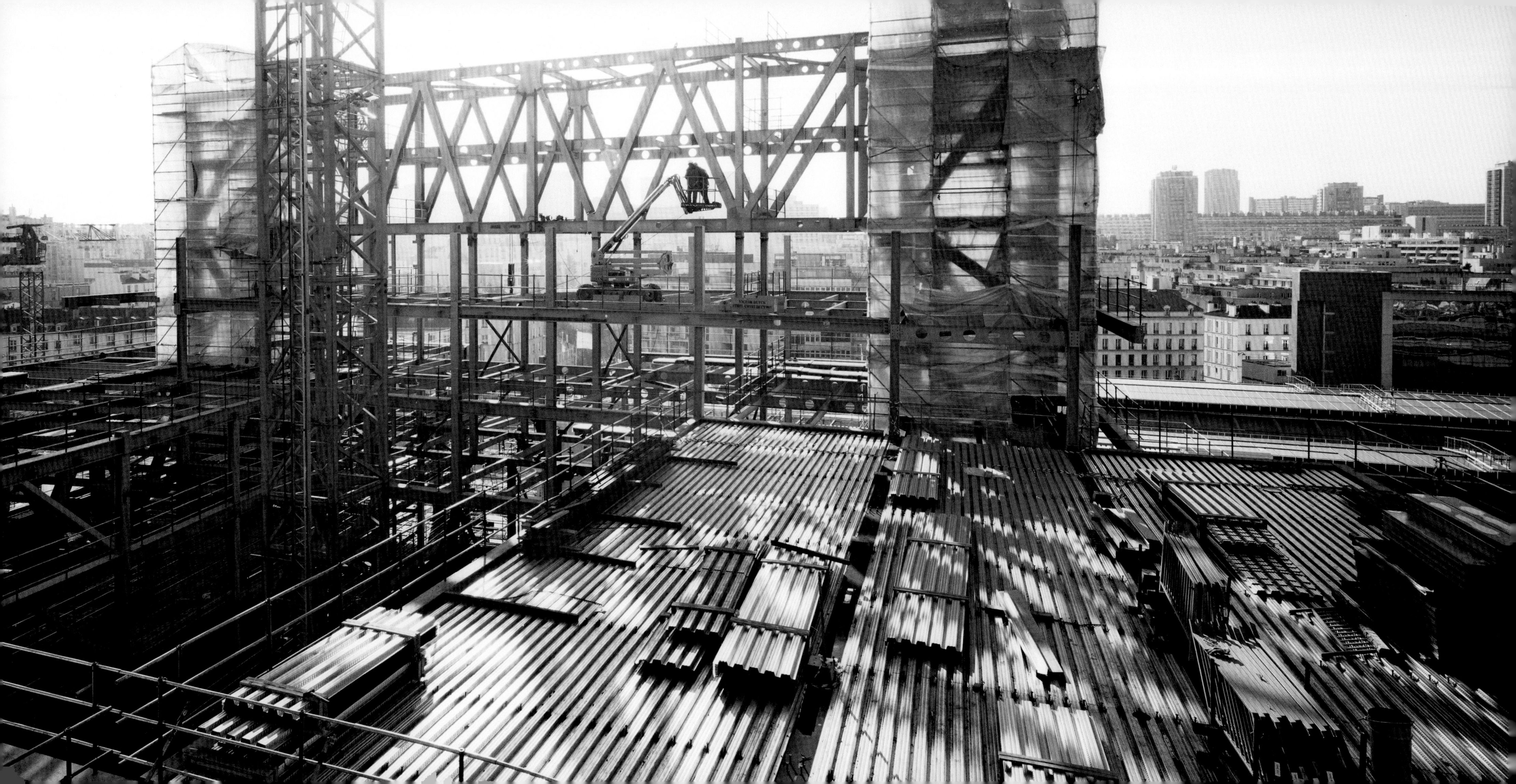

April 2017

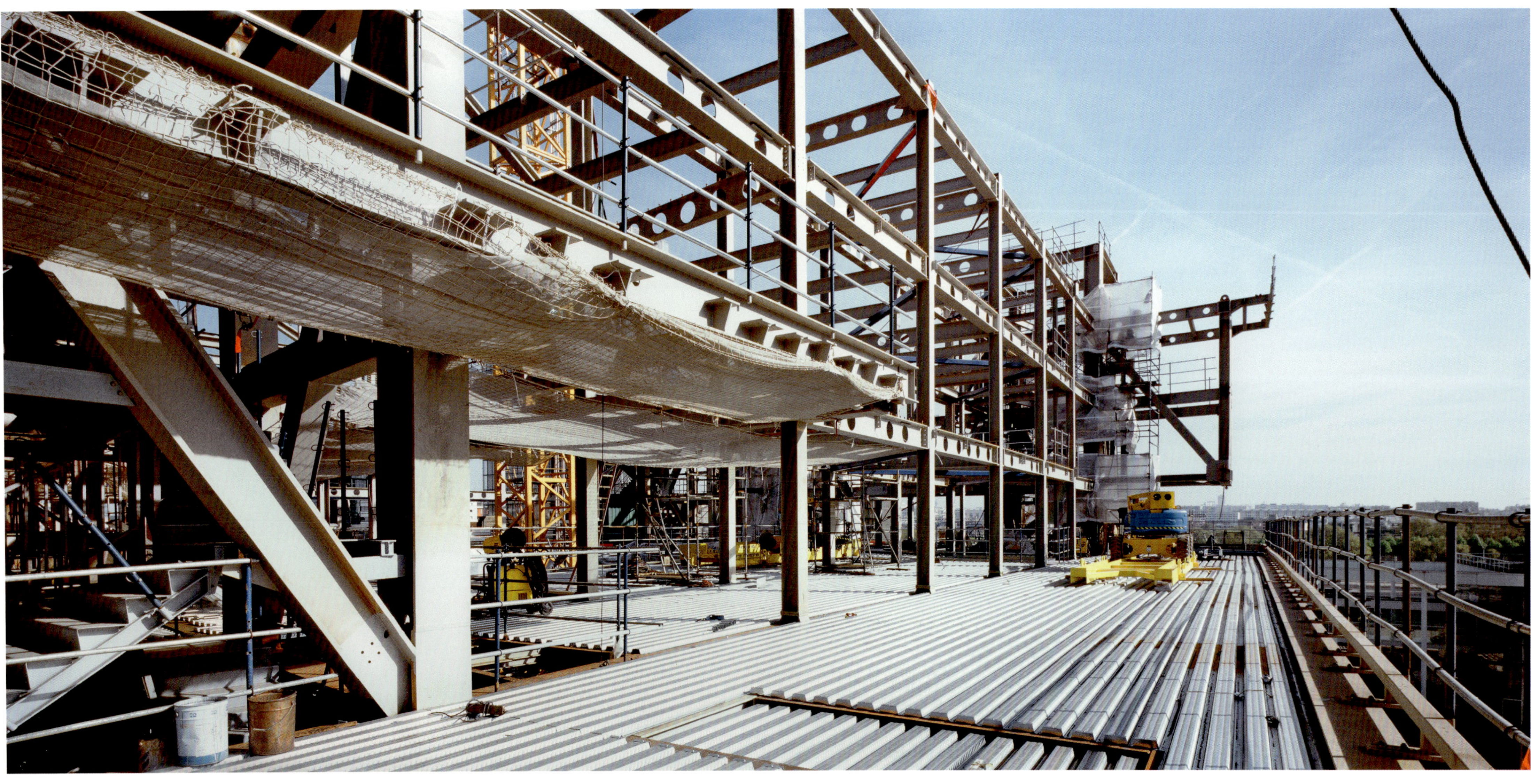

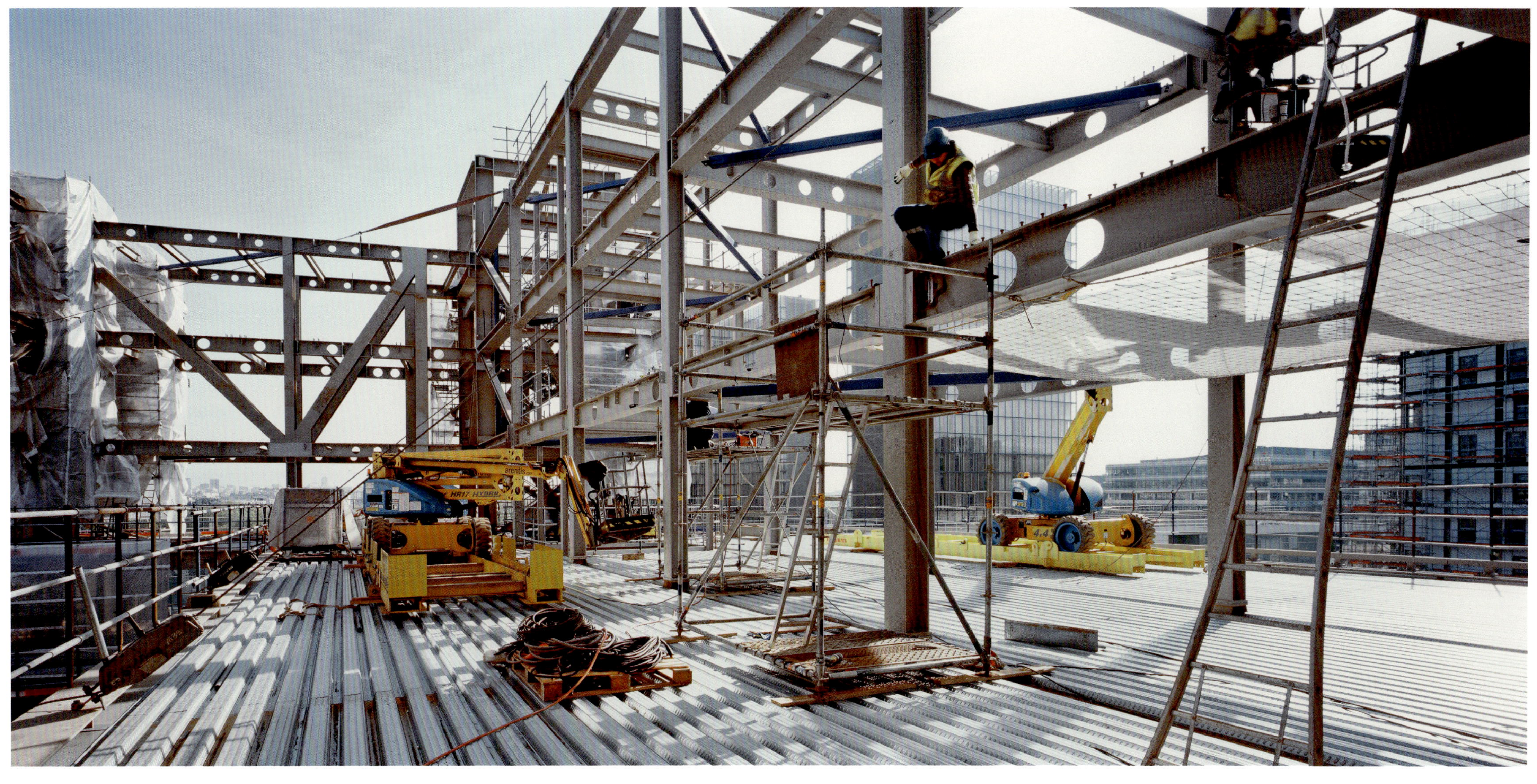

April 2017

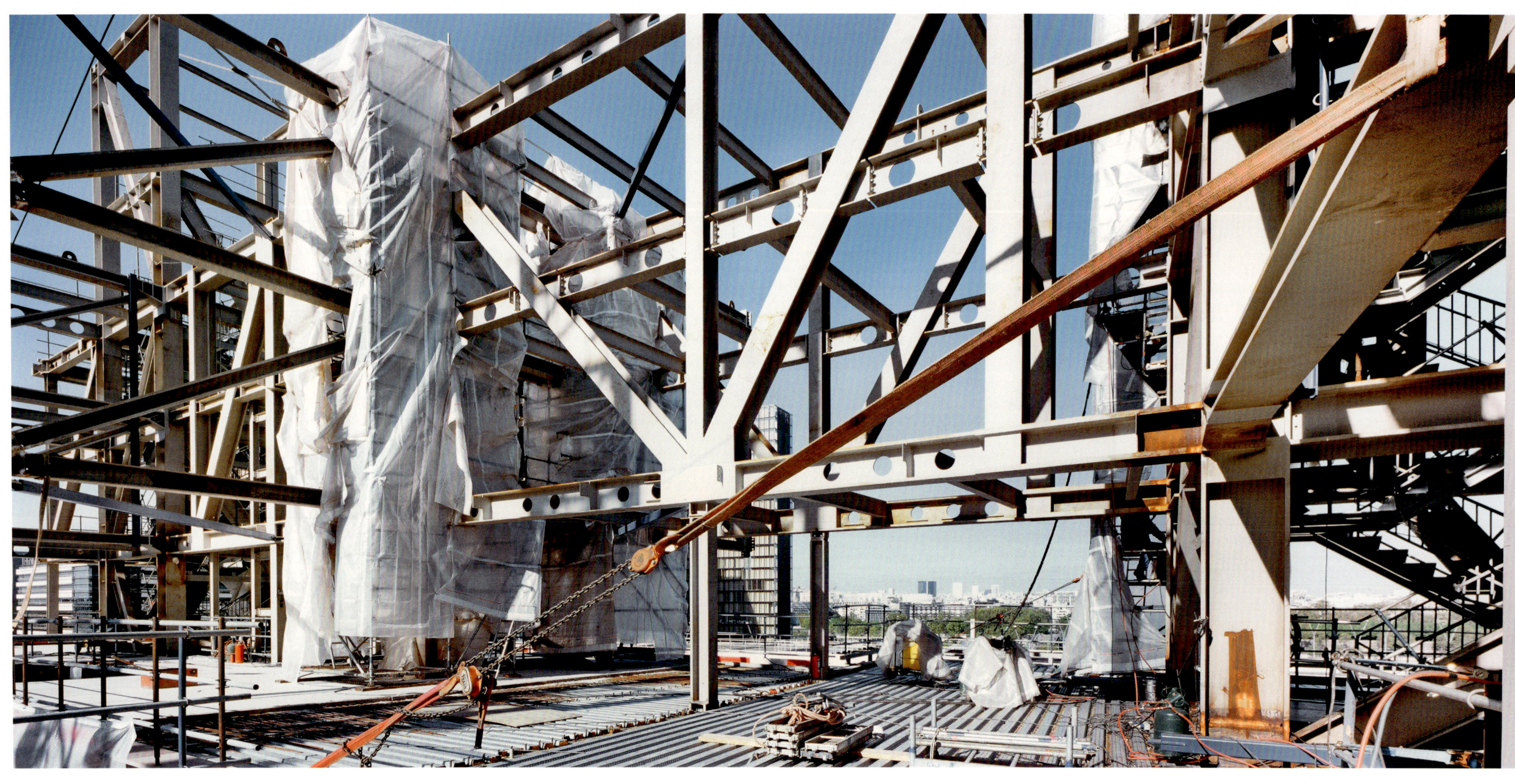

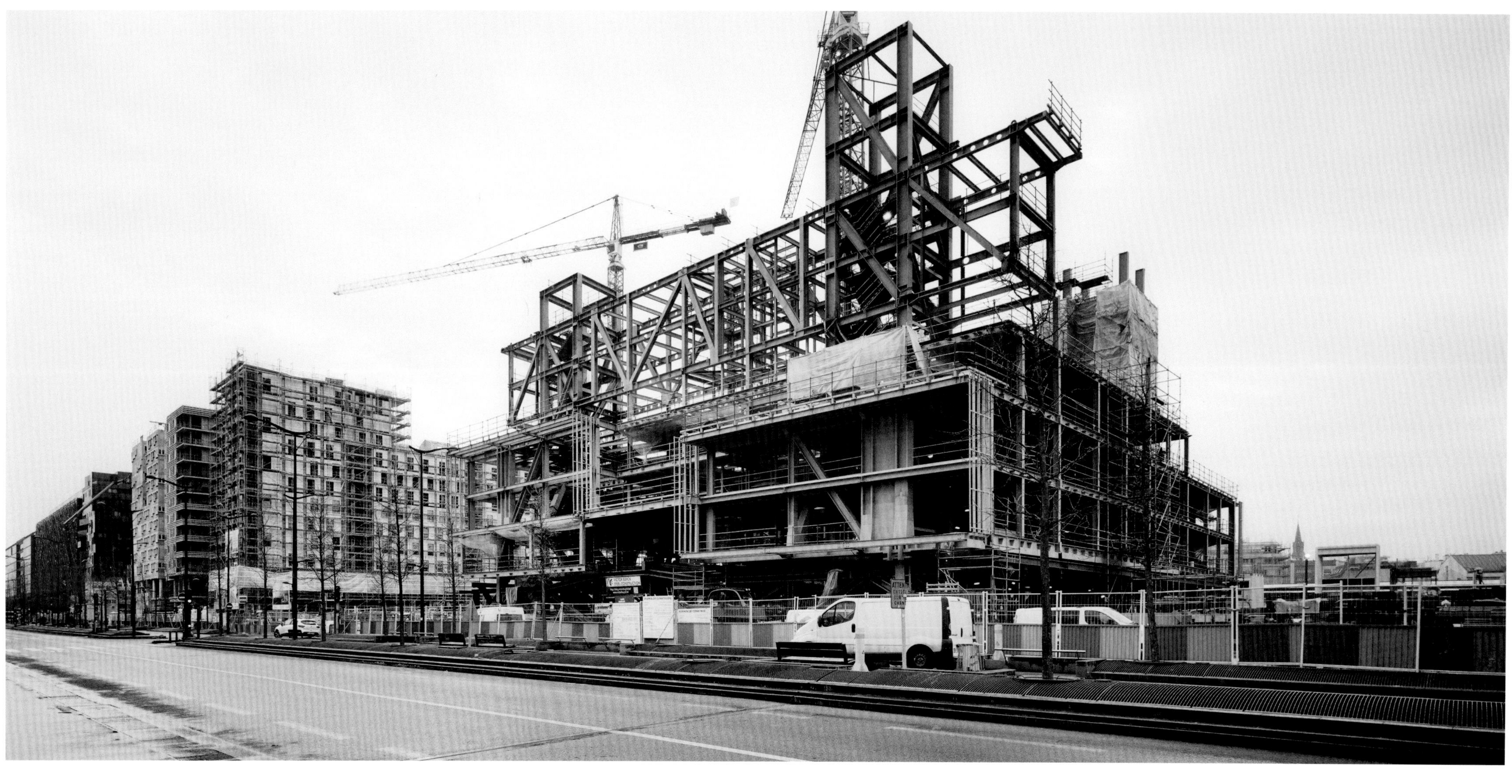

June 2017

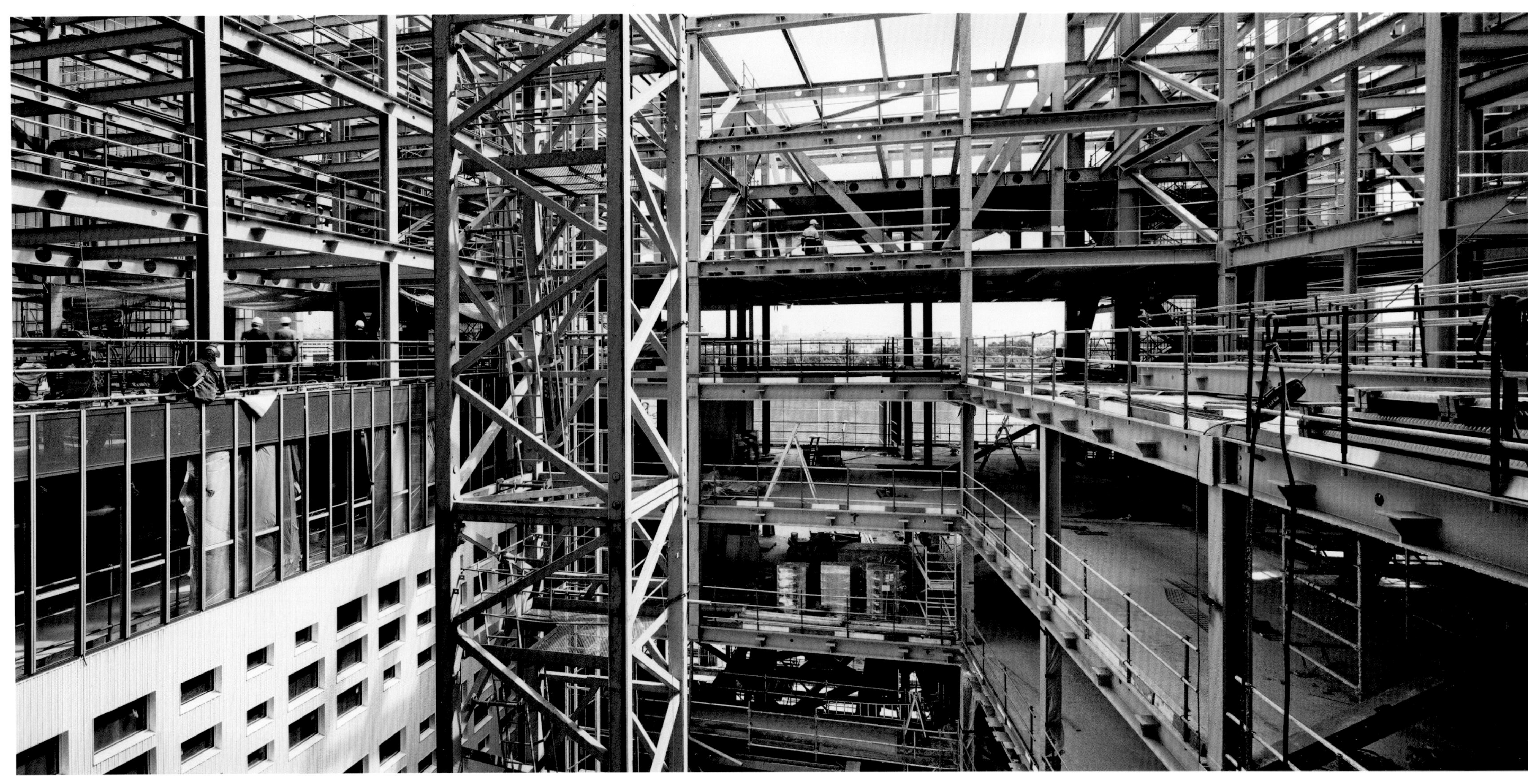

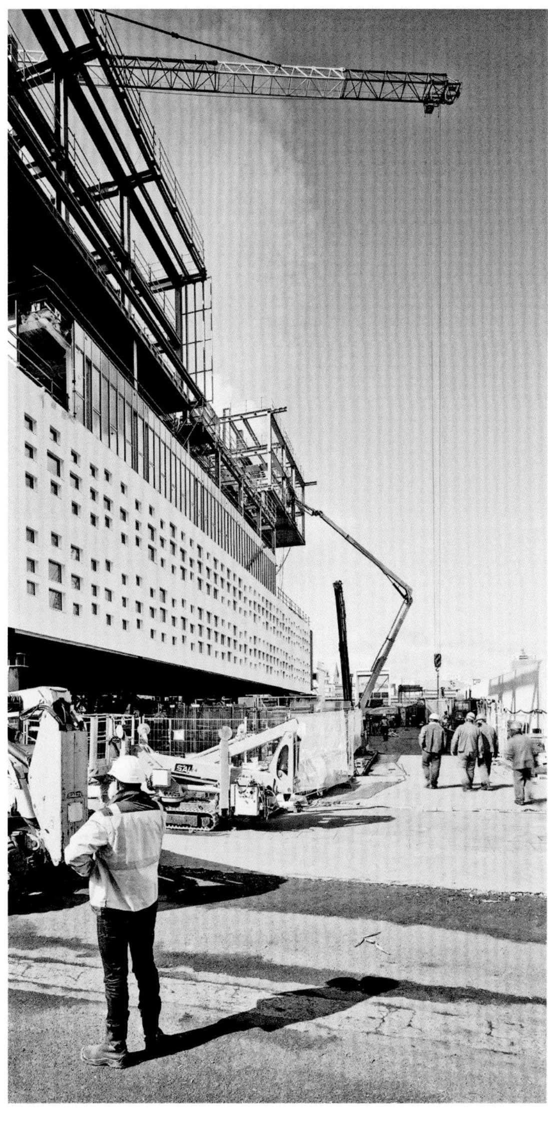

June 2017

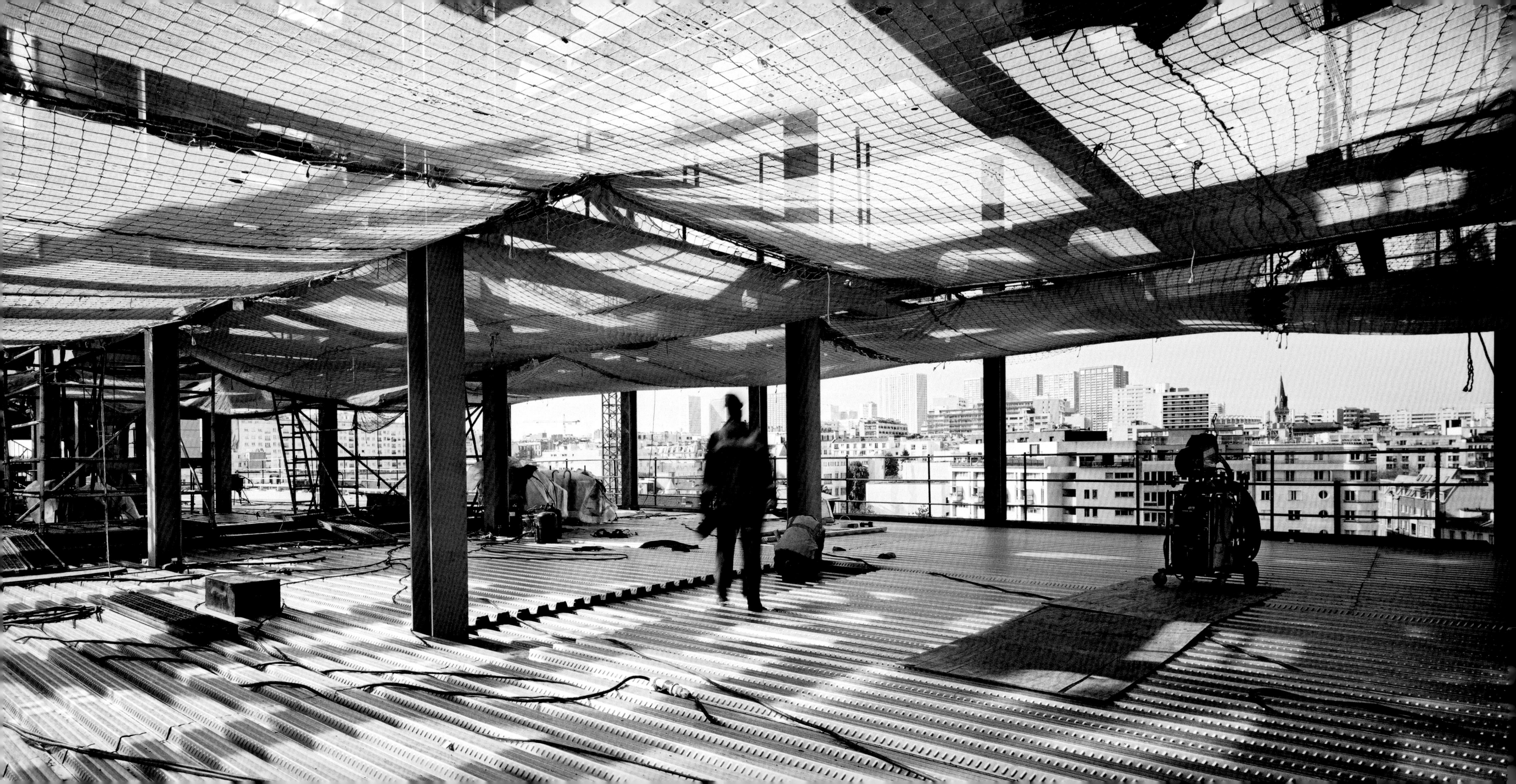

September 2017

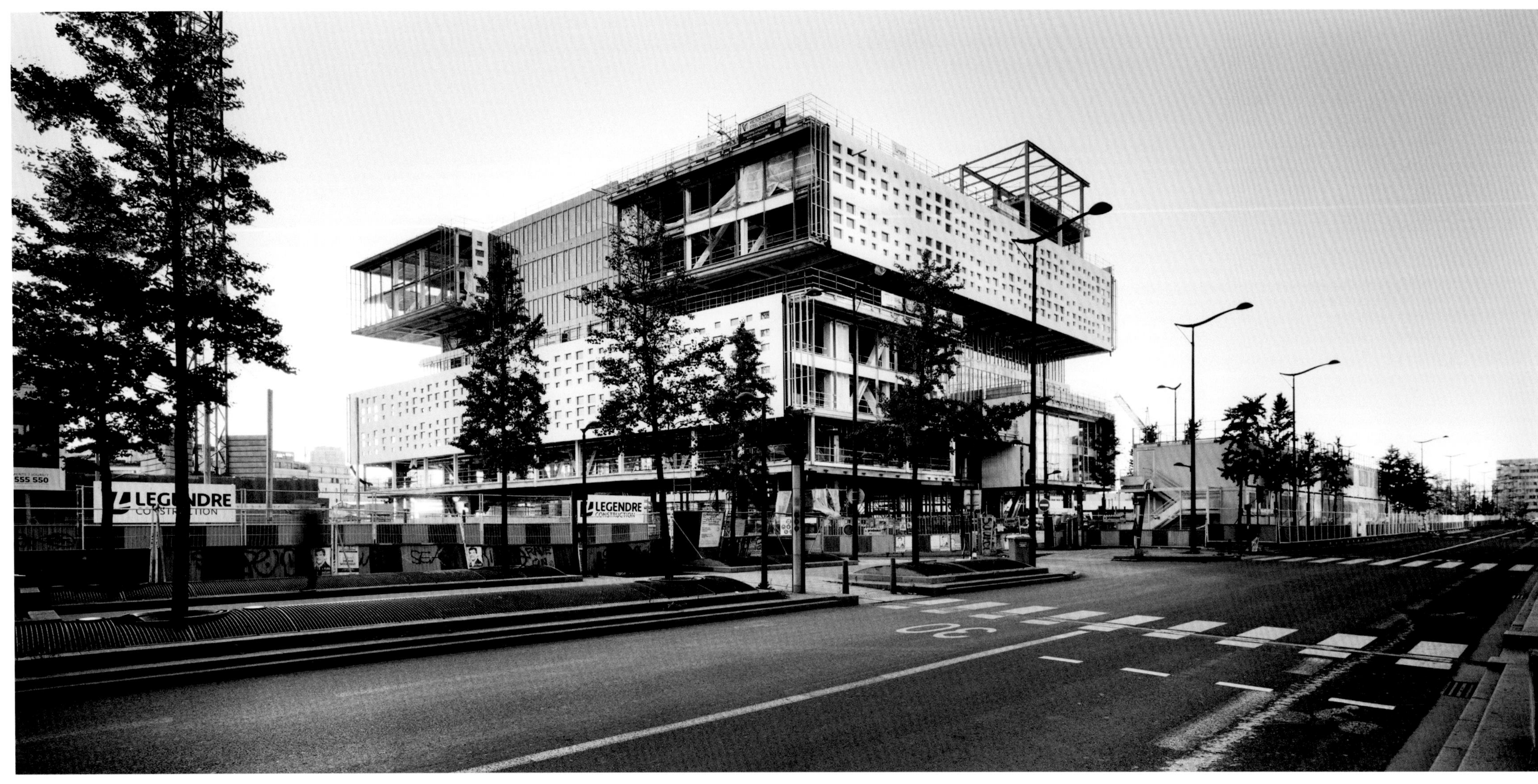

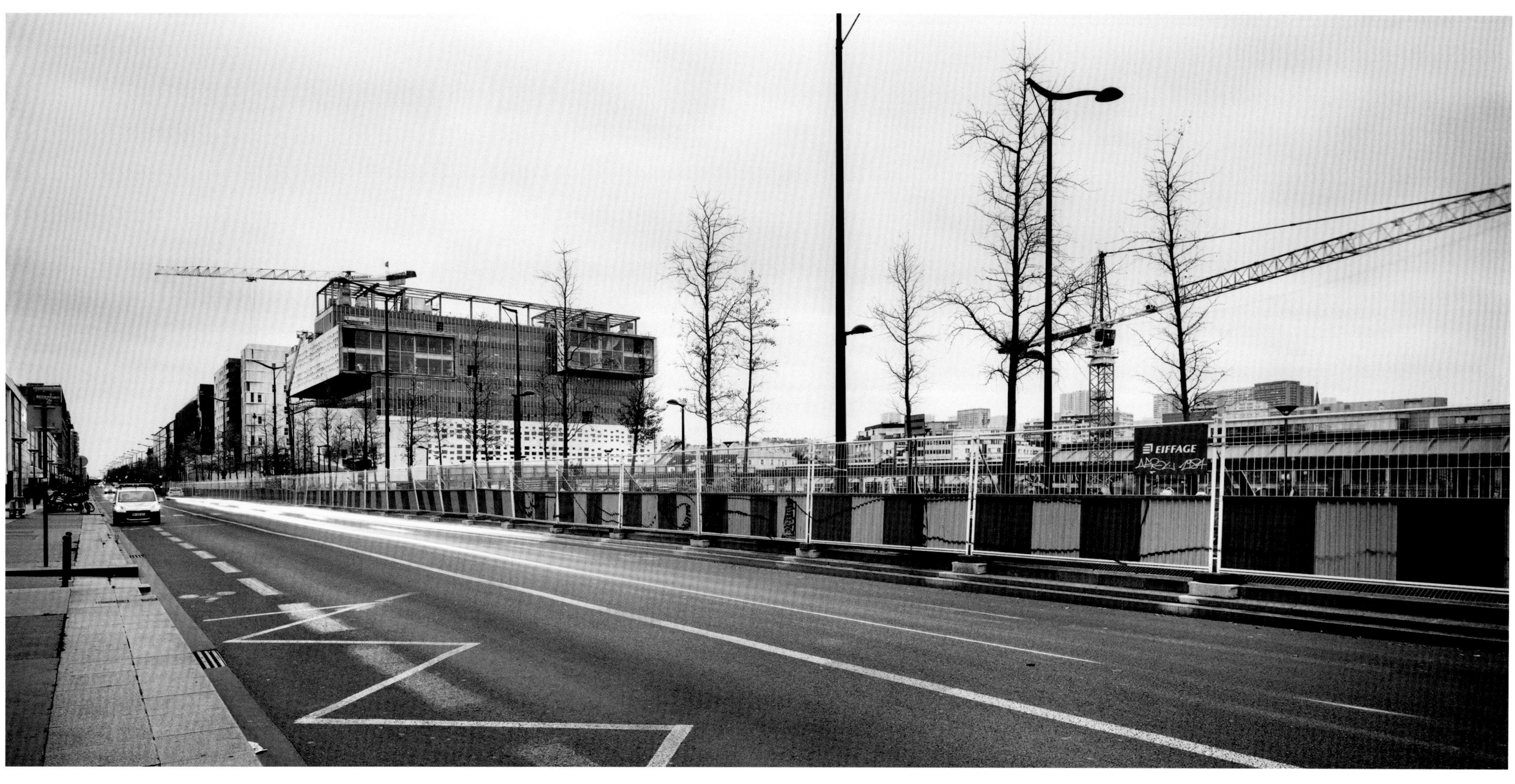
EIFFAGE

November 2017

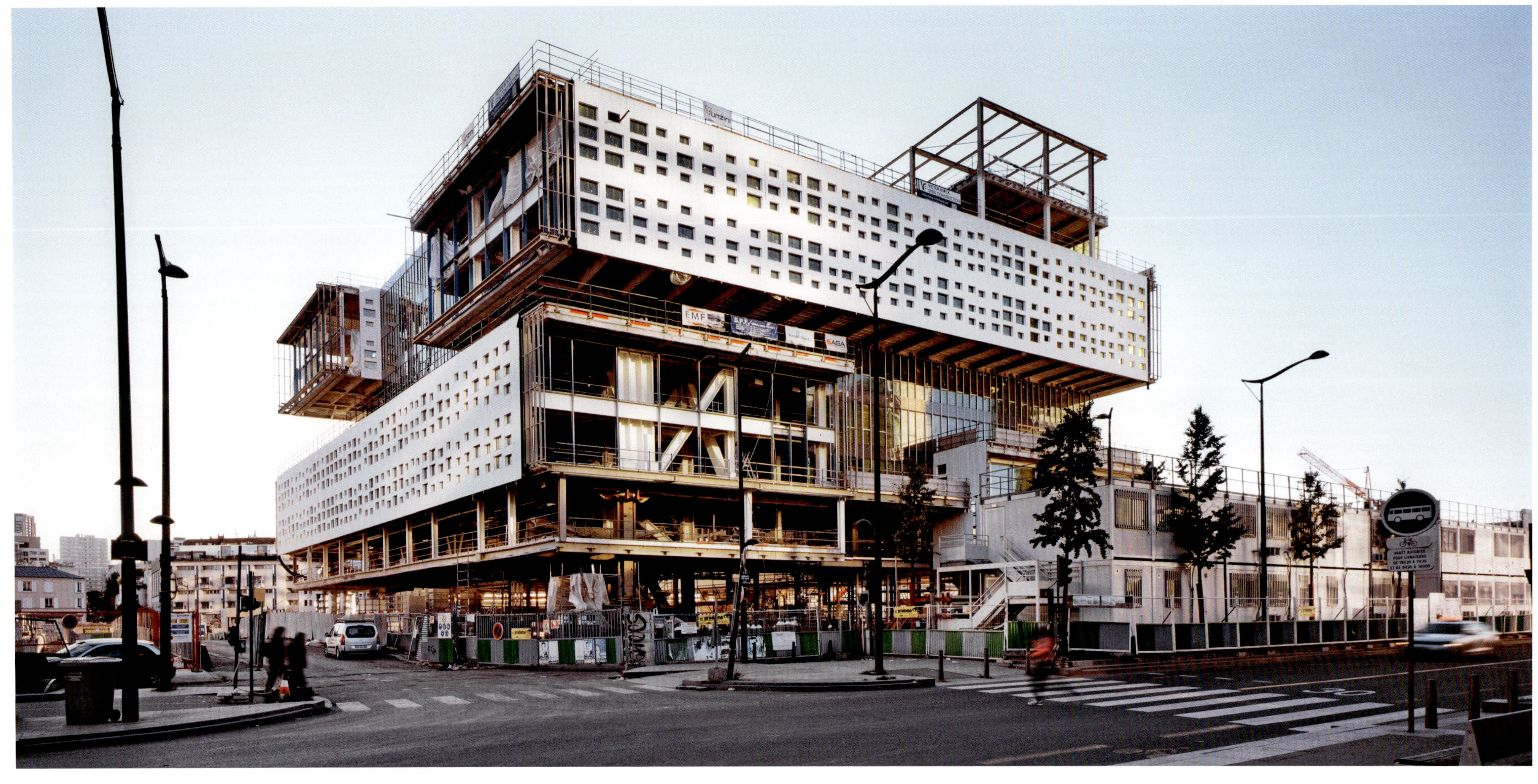

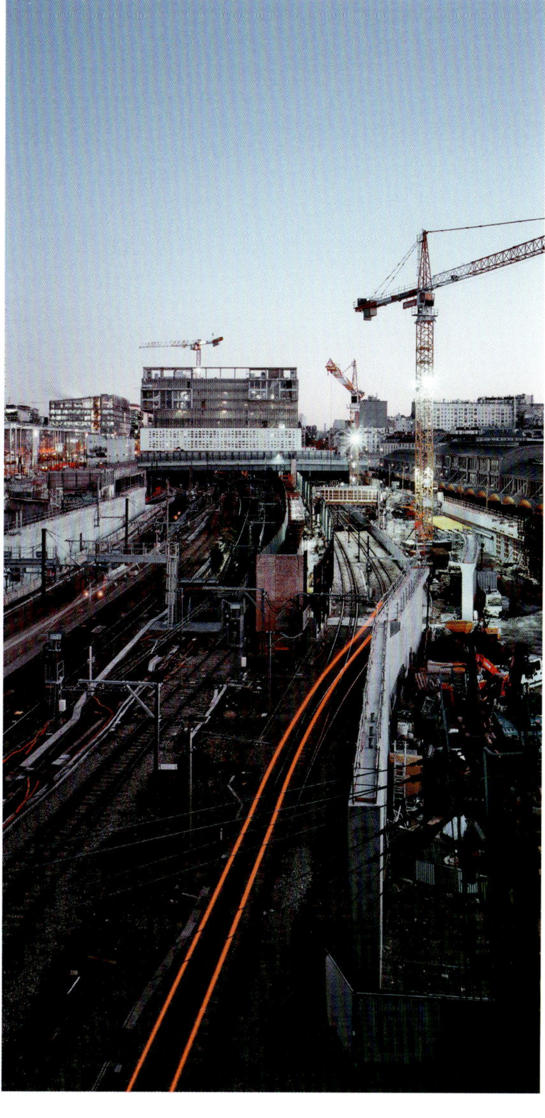

May 2019

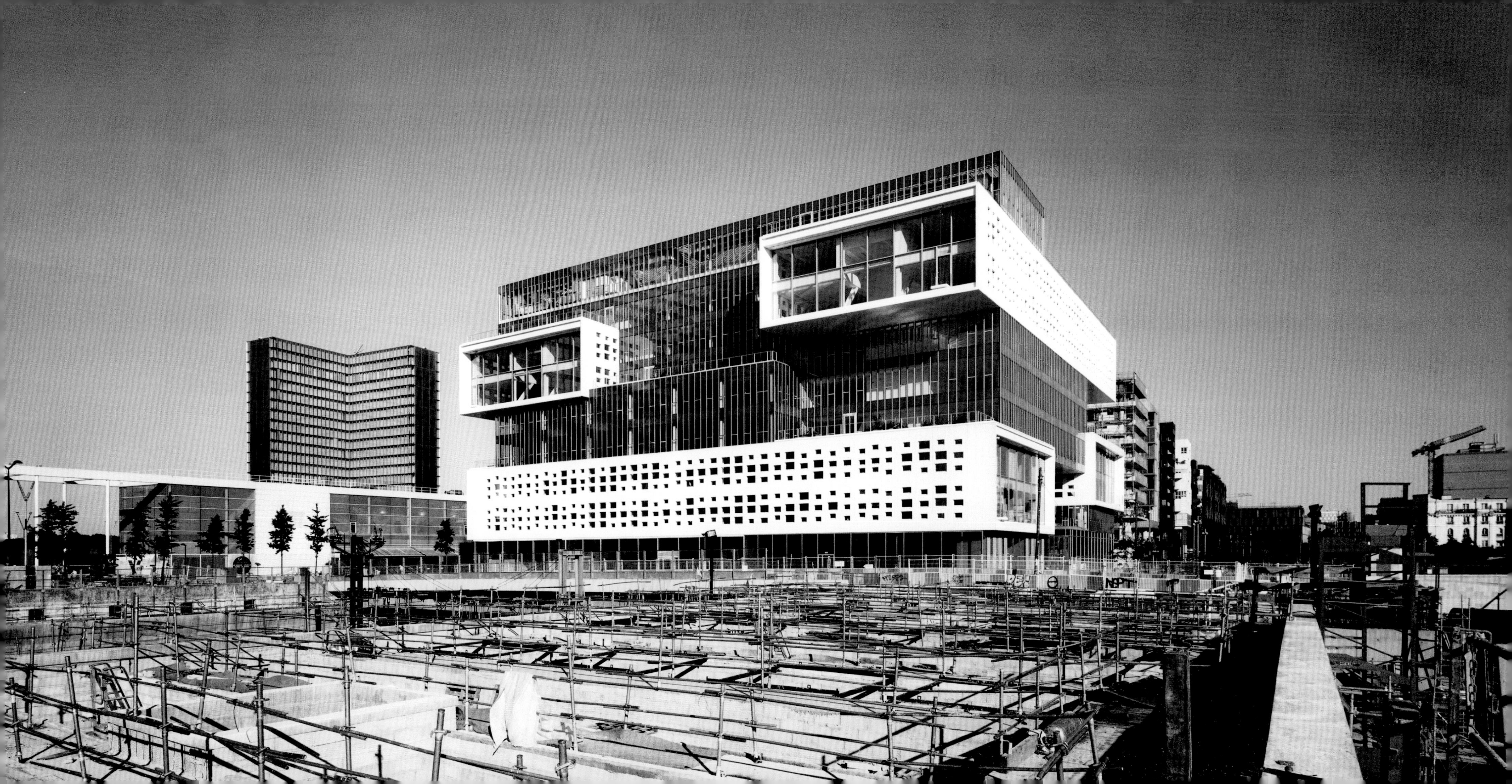

July 2018

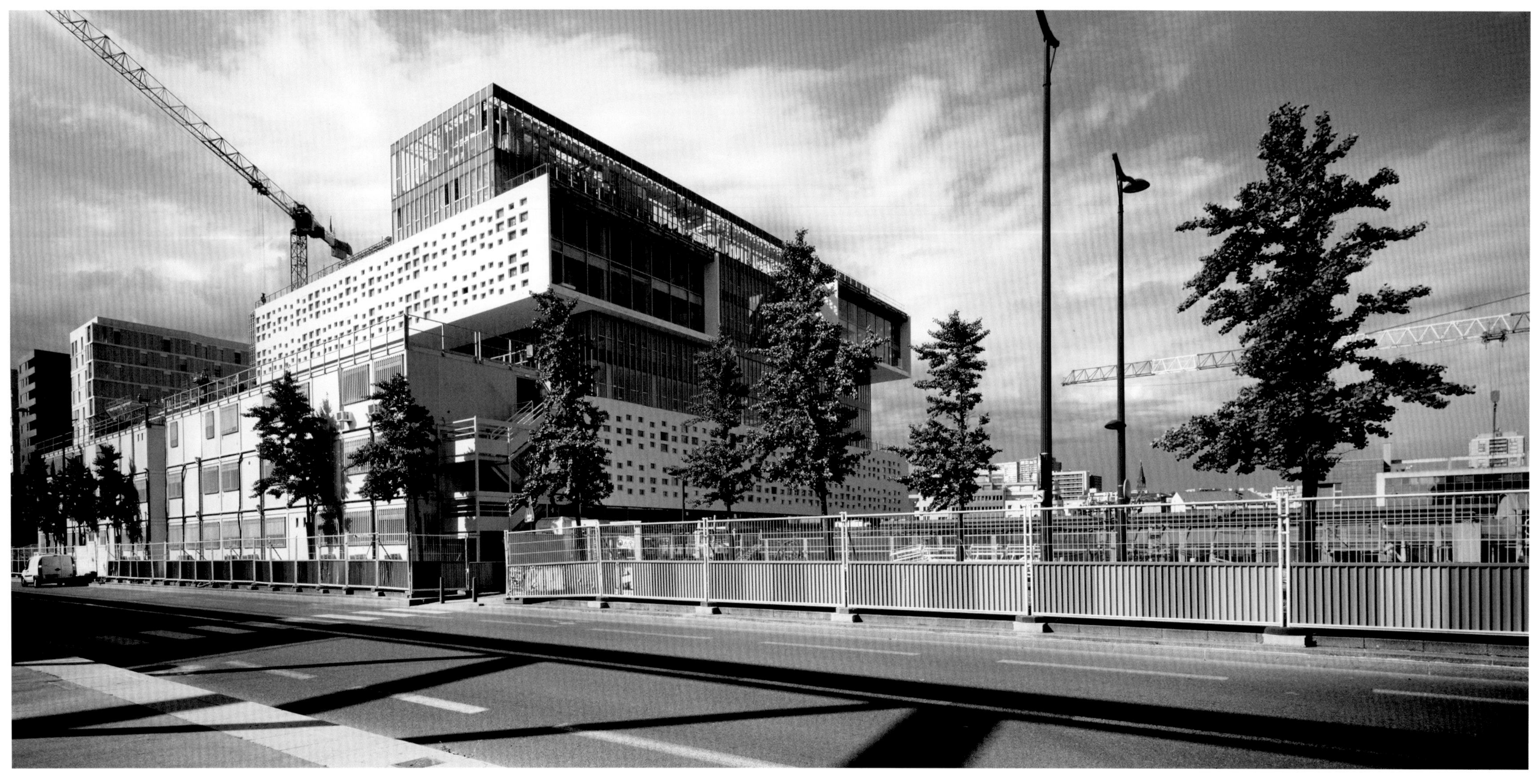

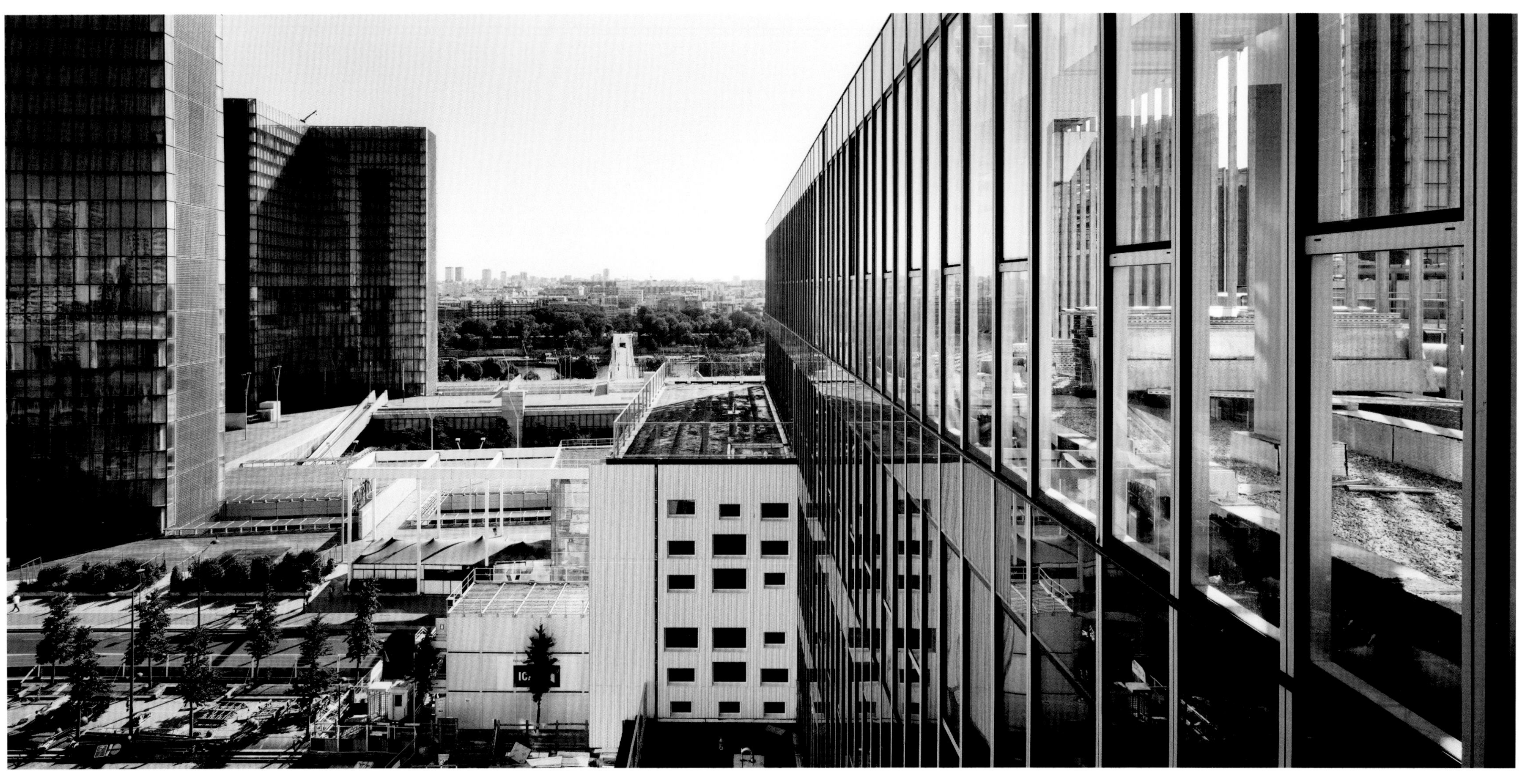

November 2017

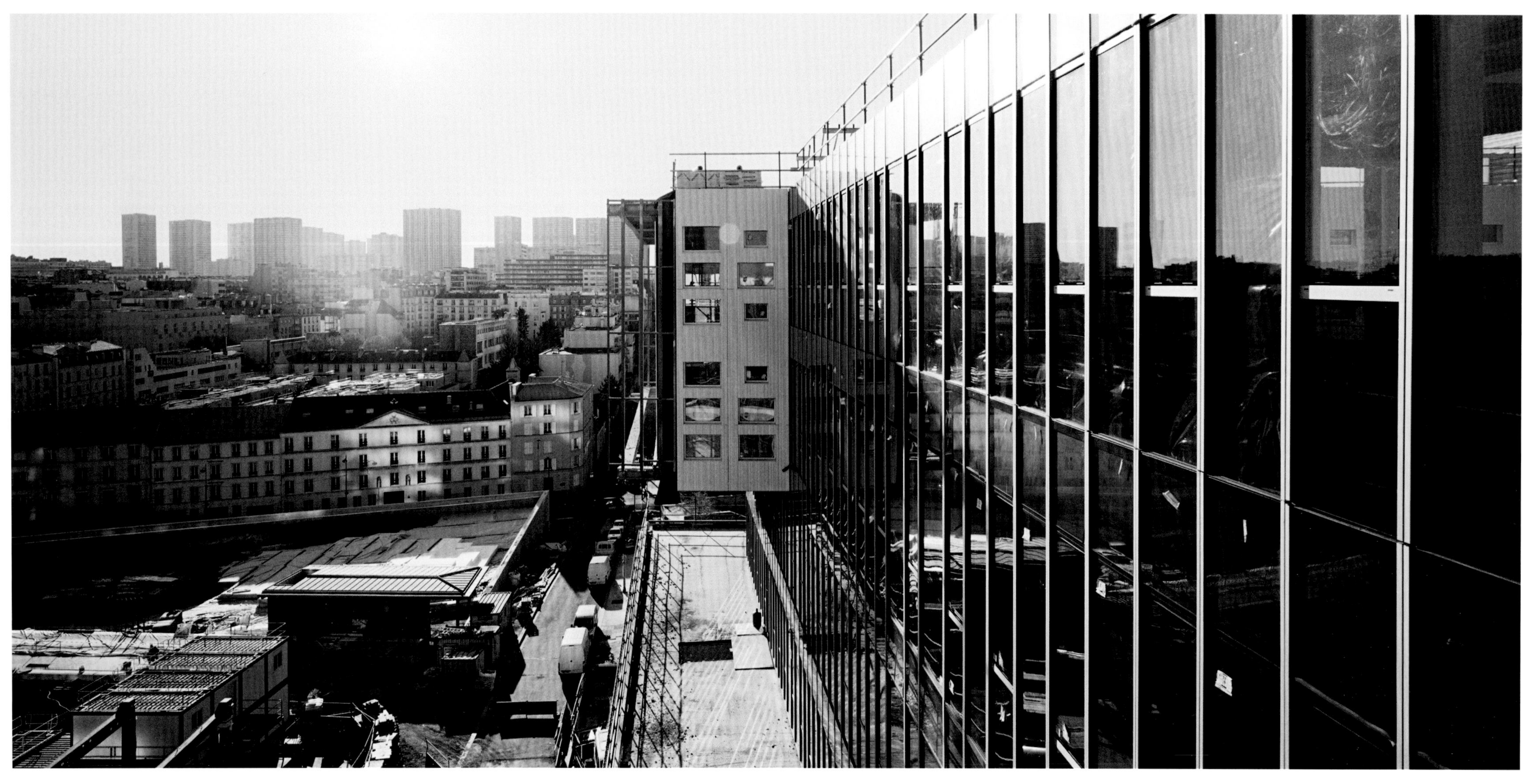

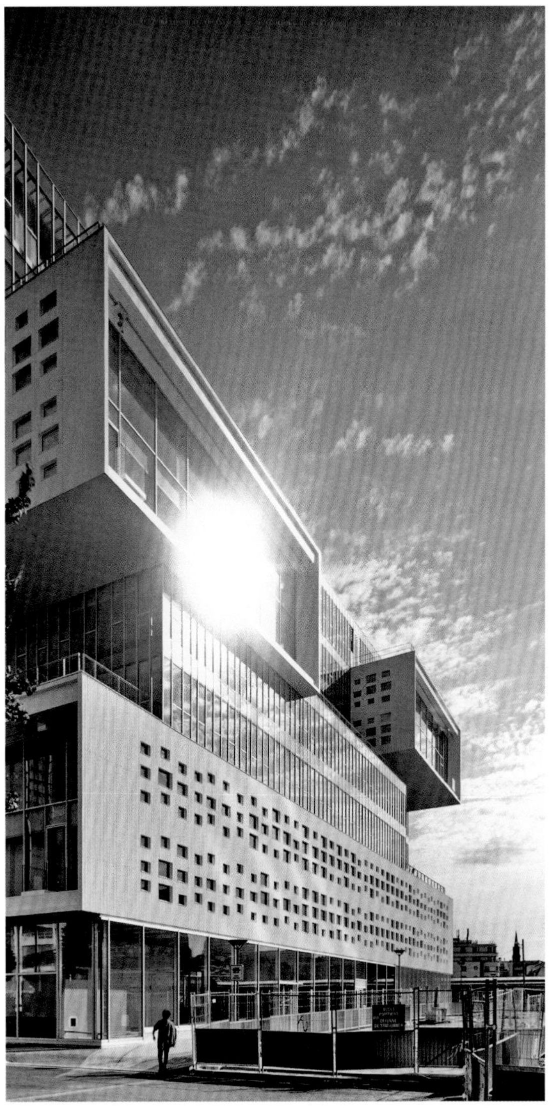

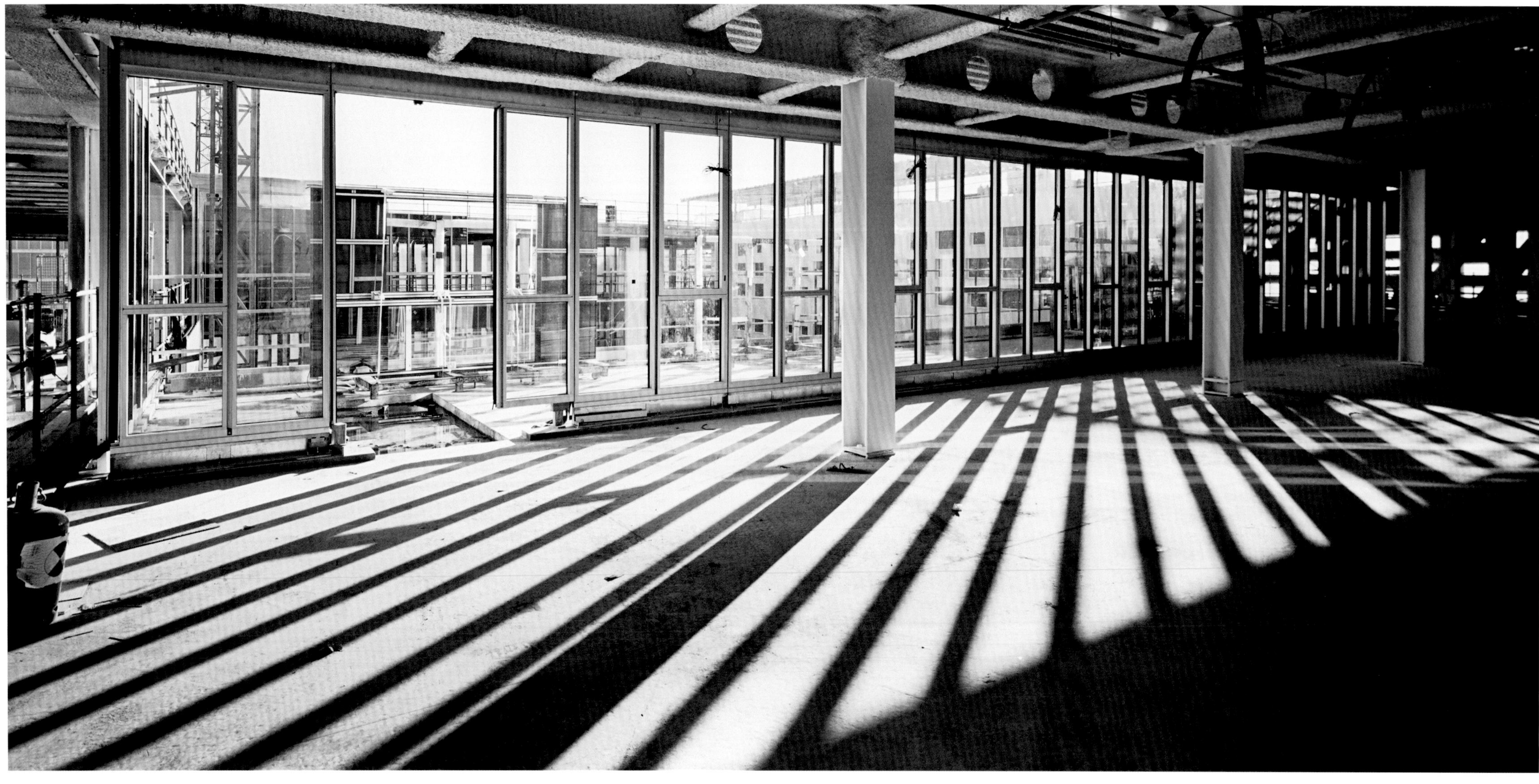

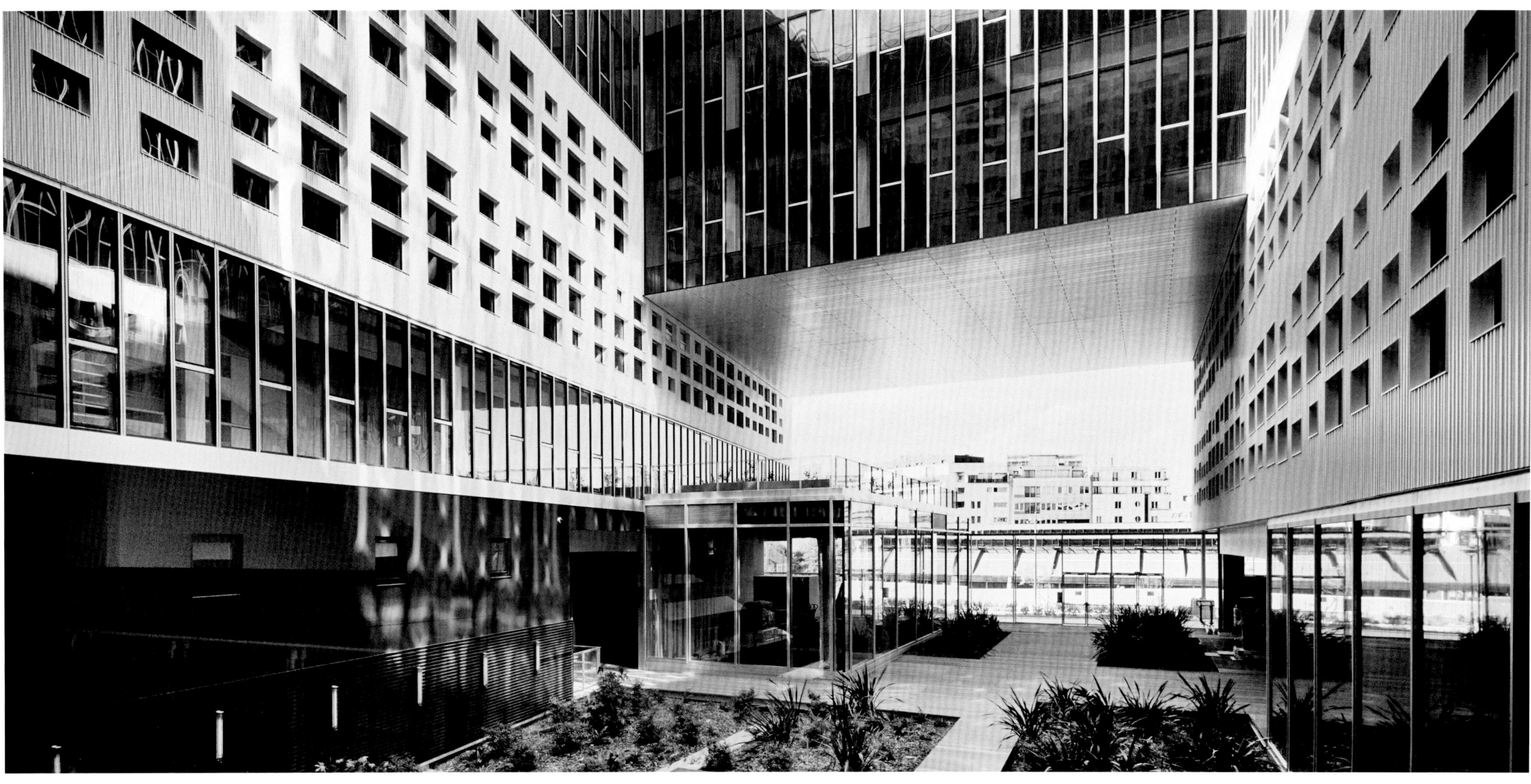

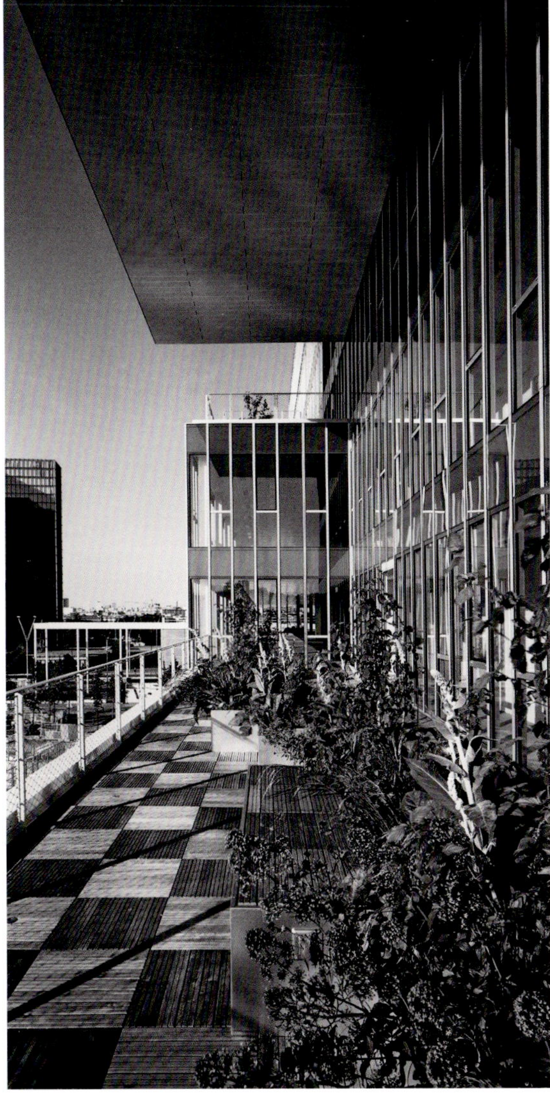

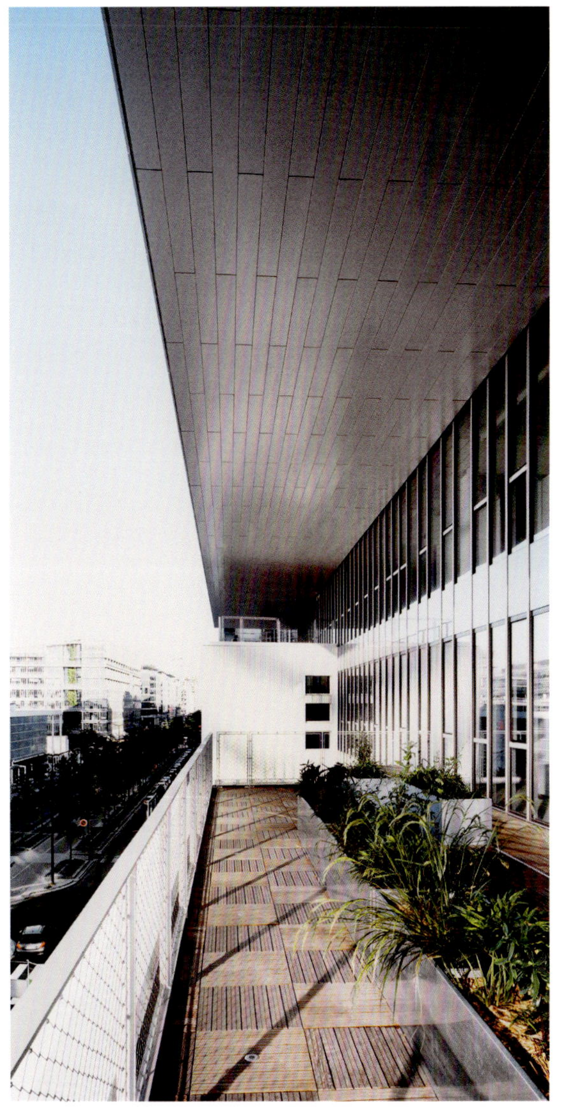

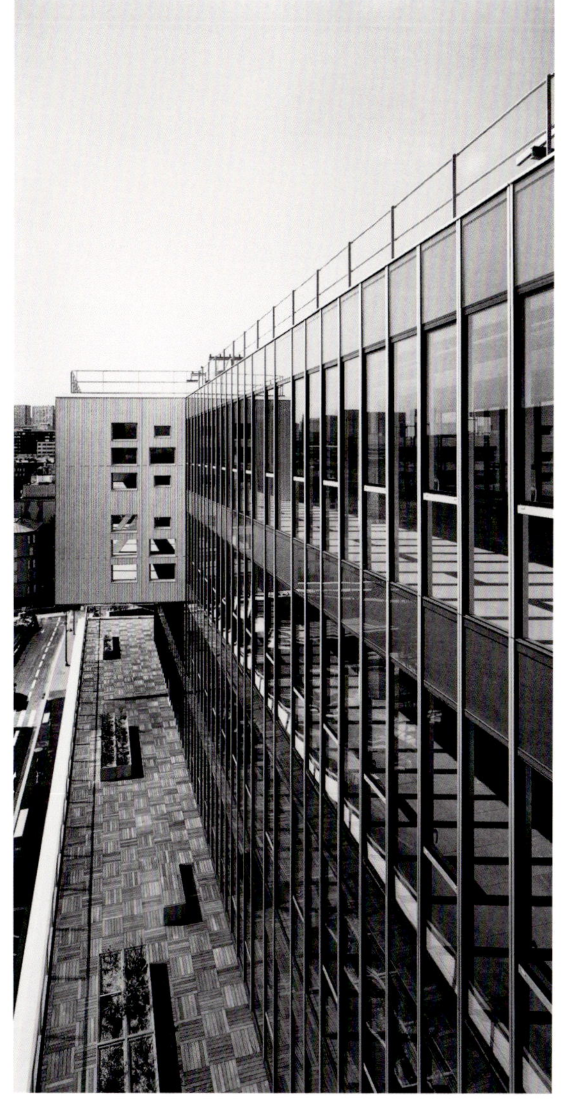

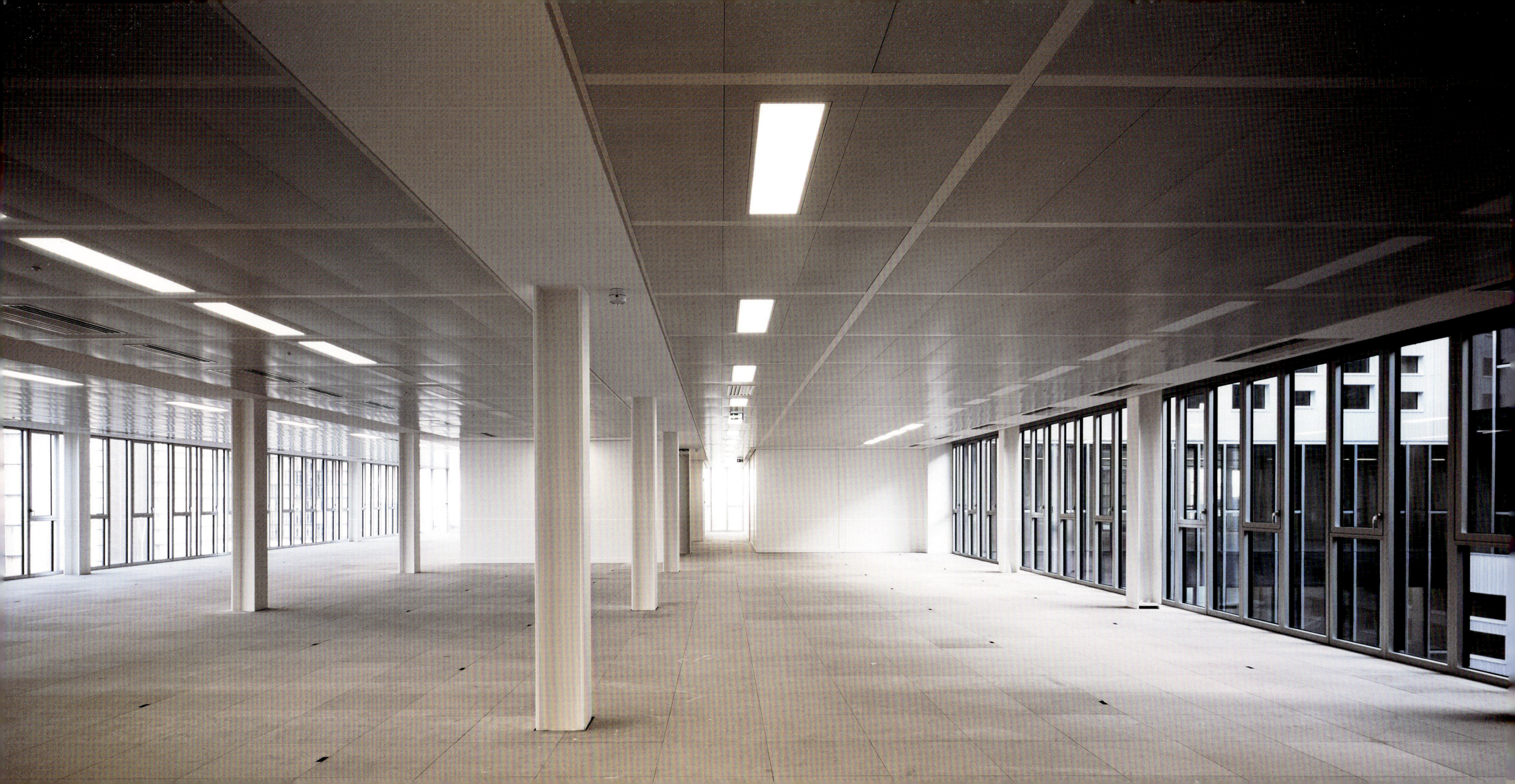

November 2018

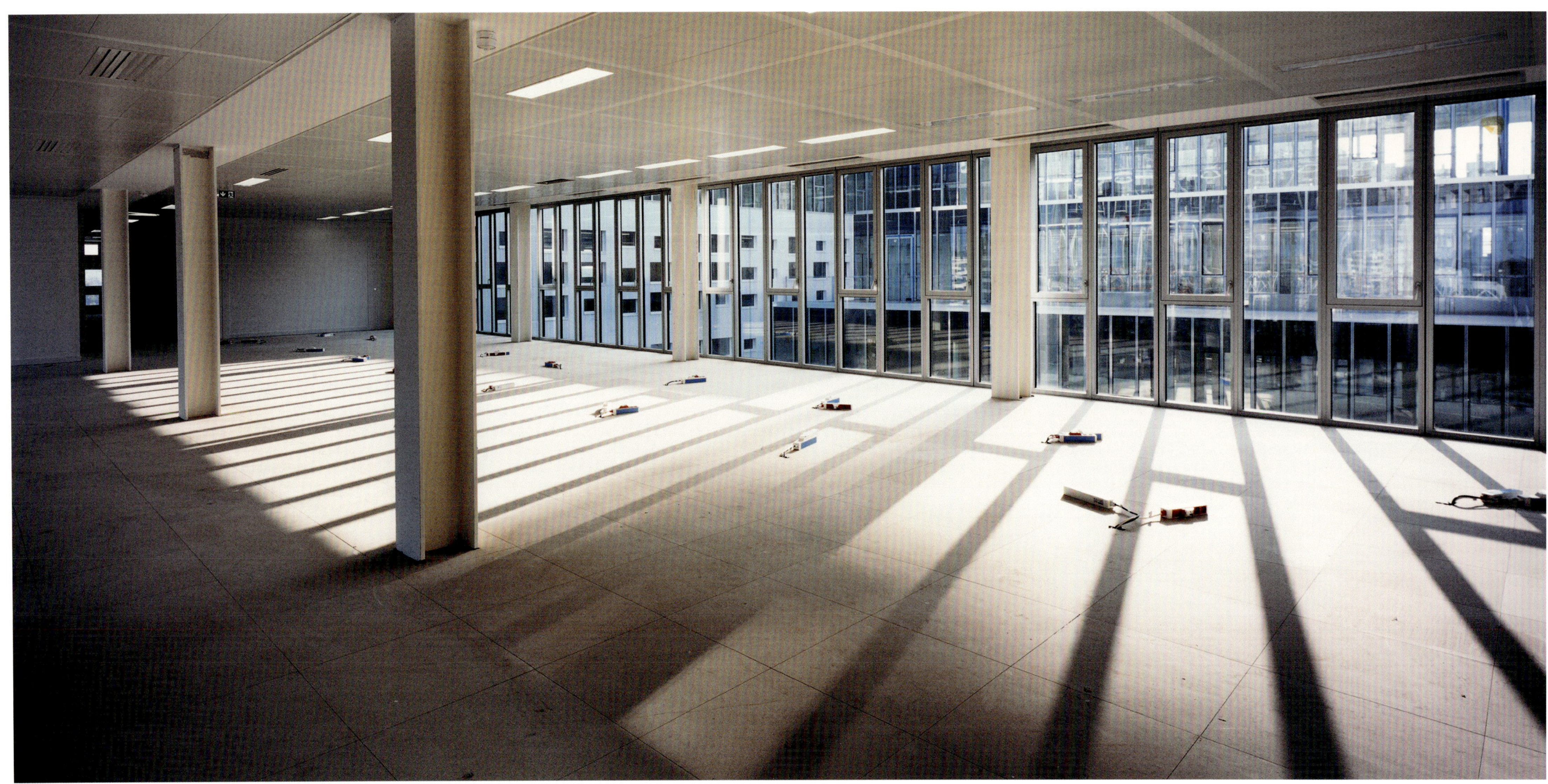

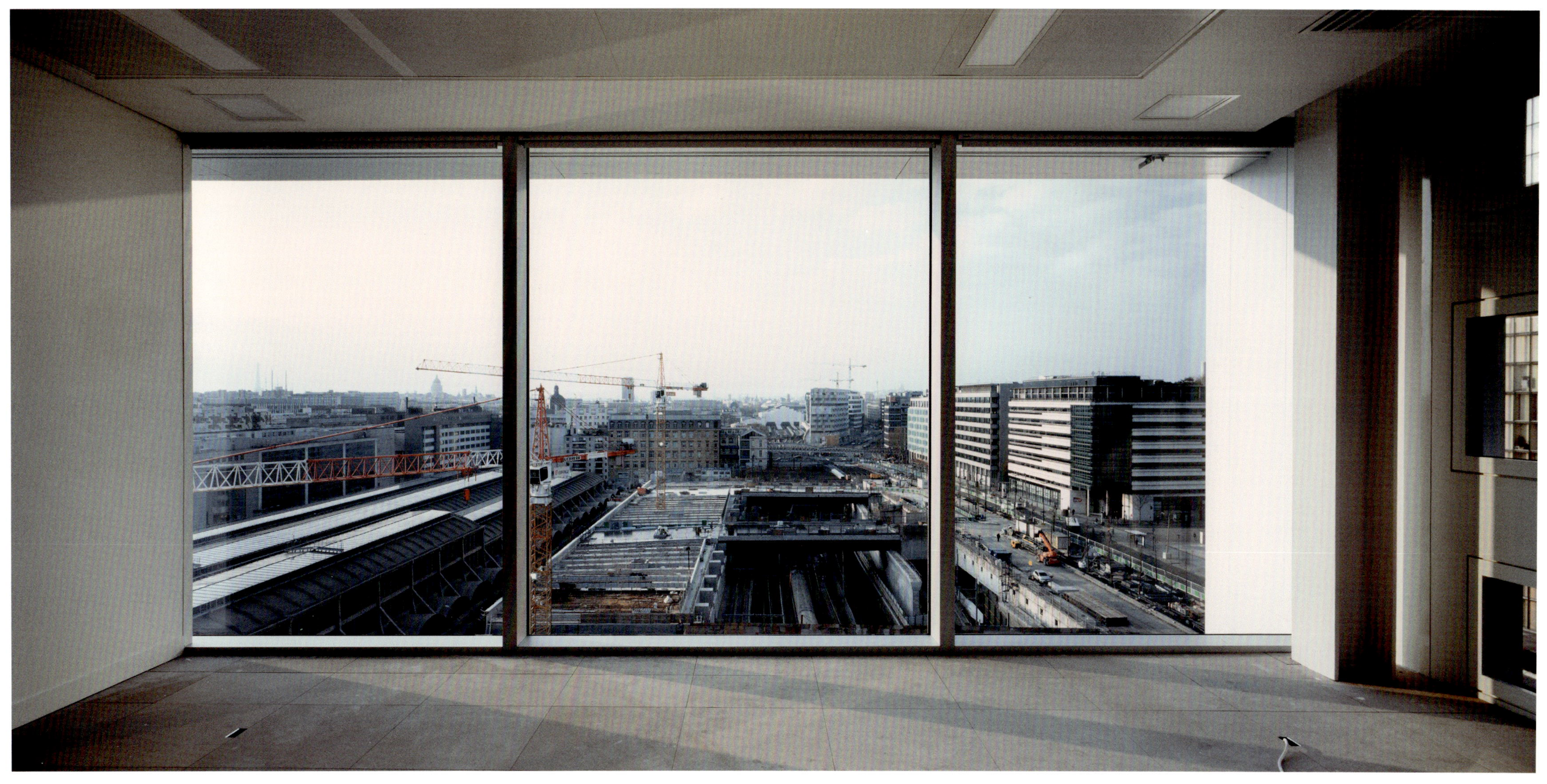

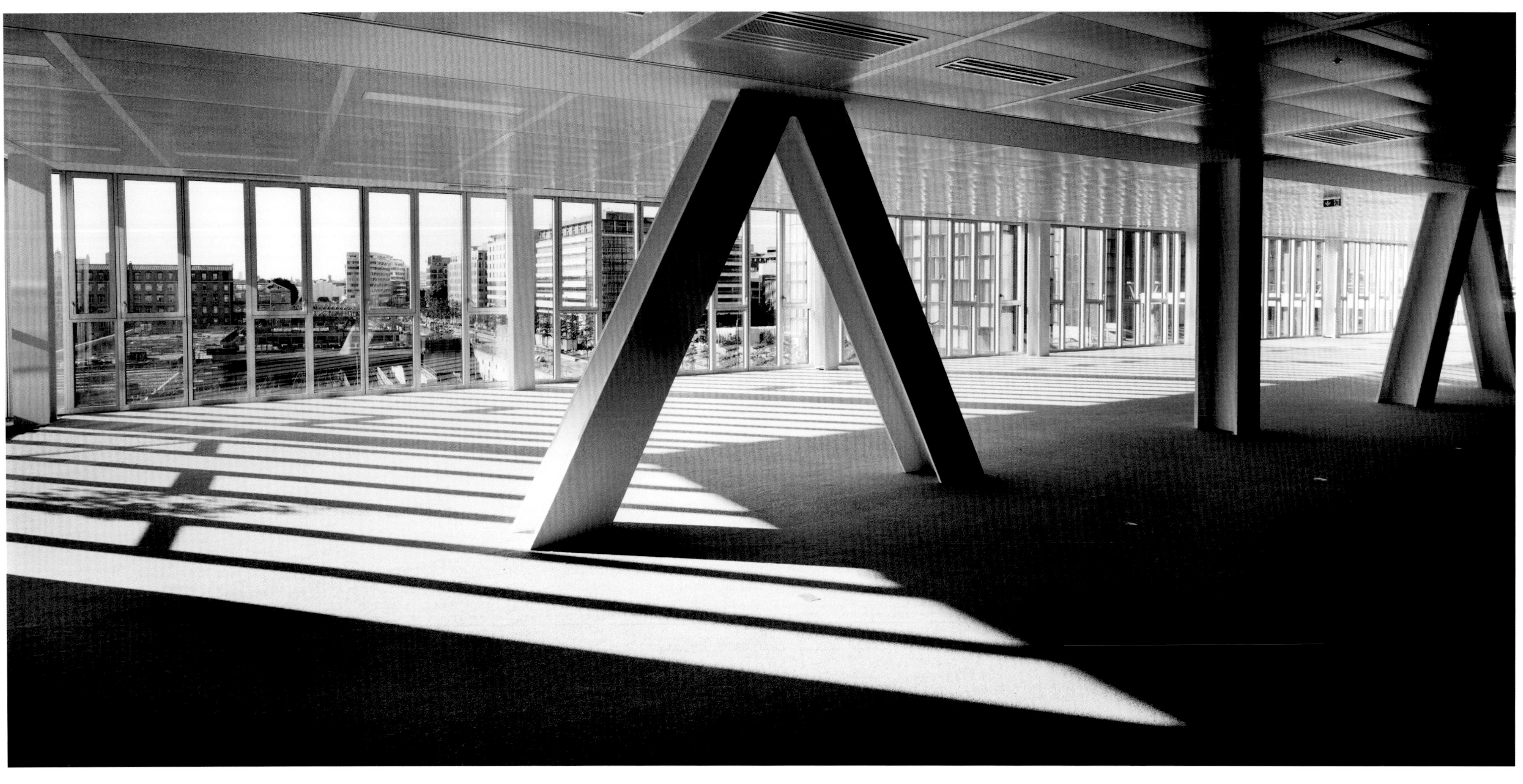

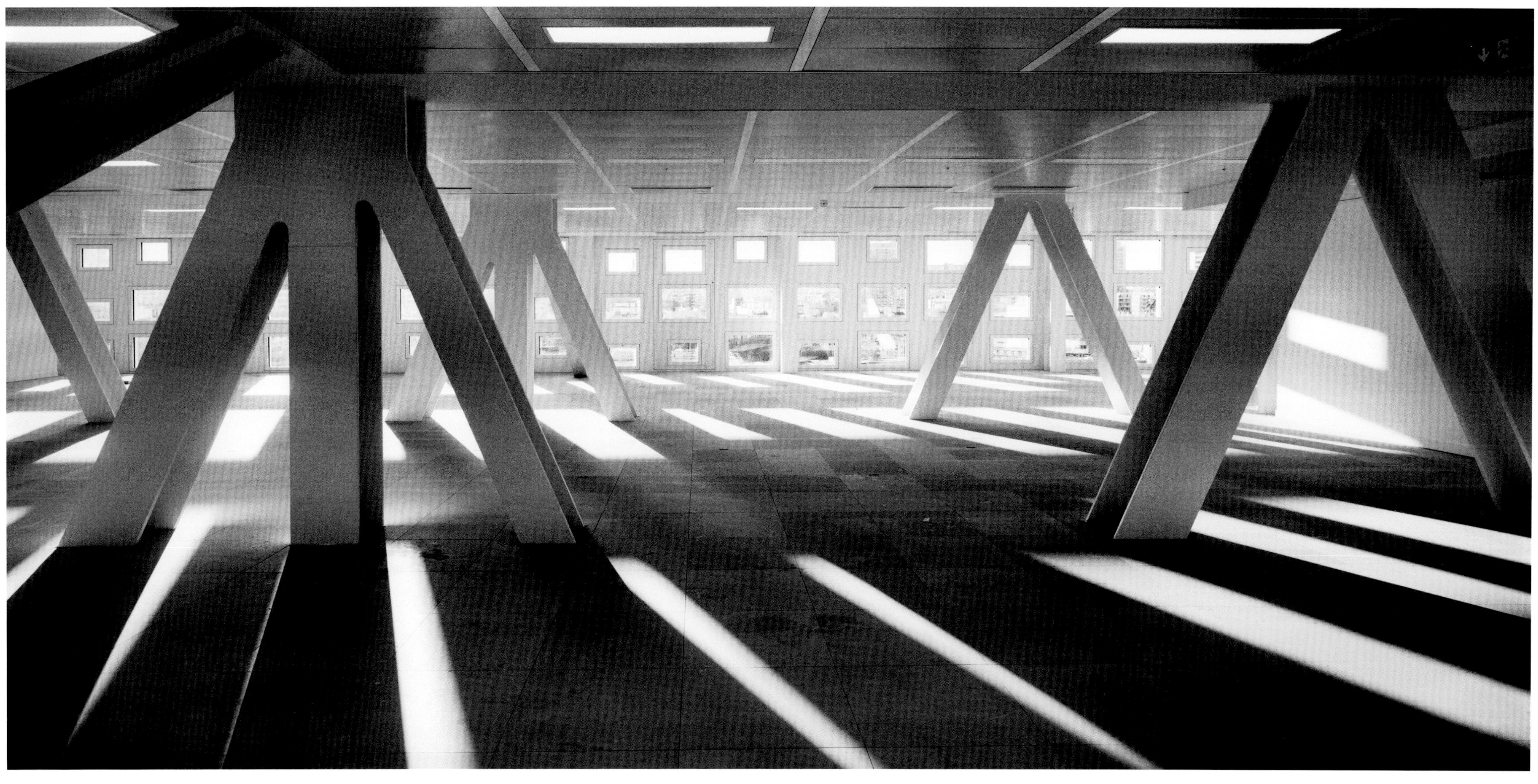

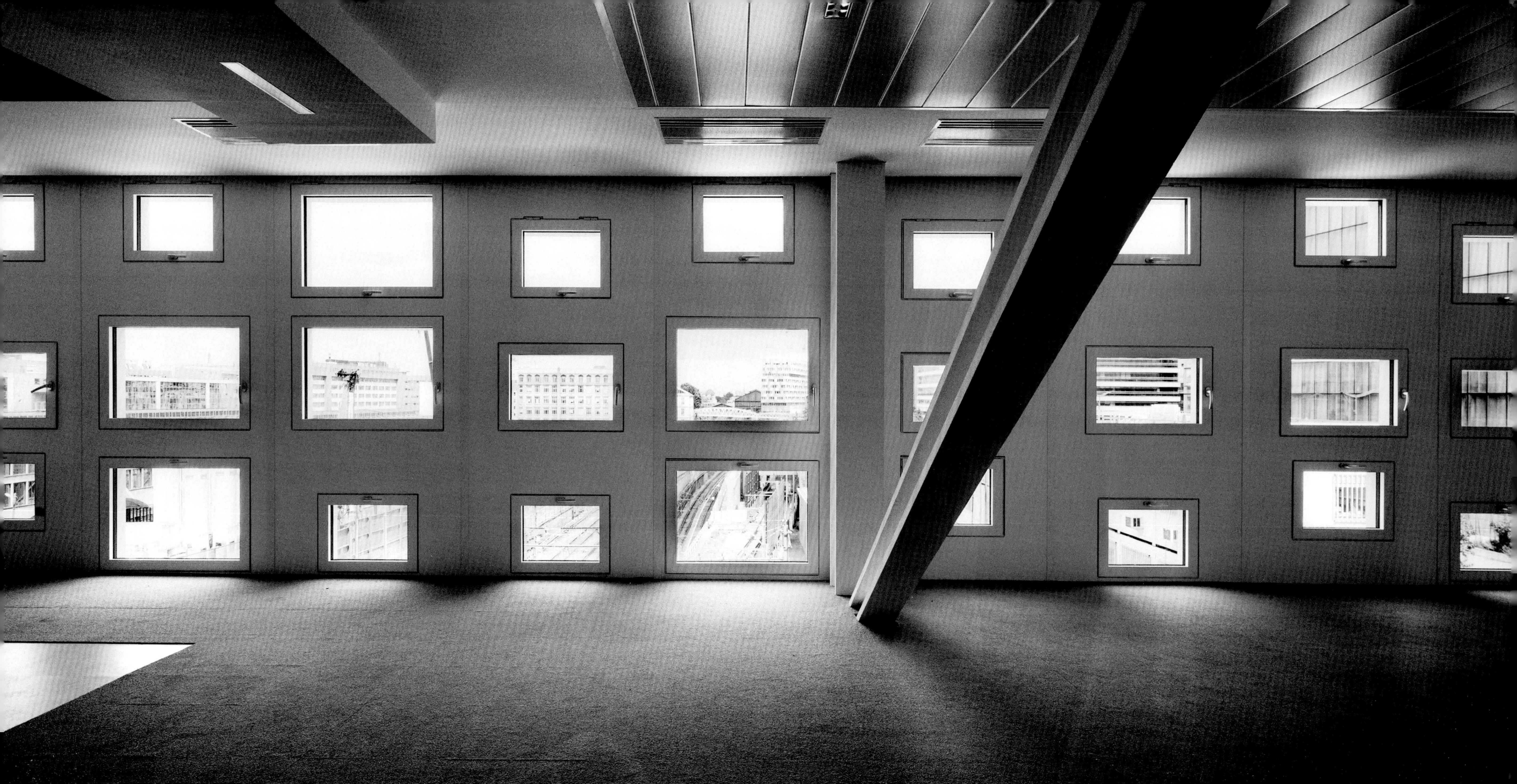

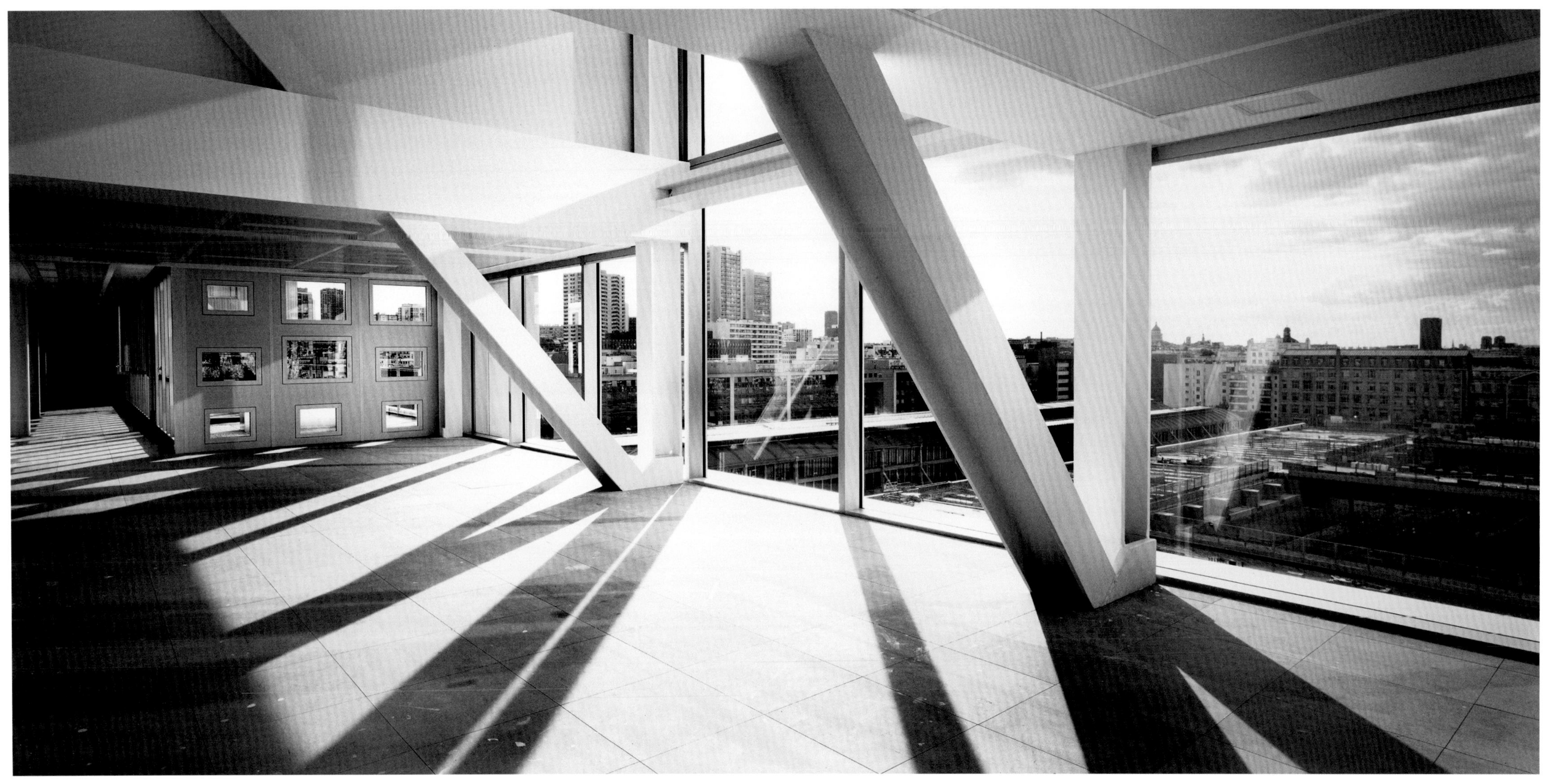

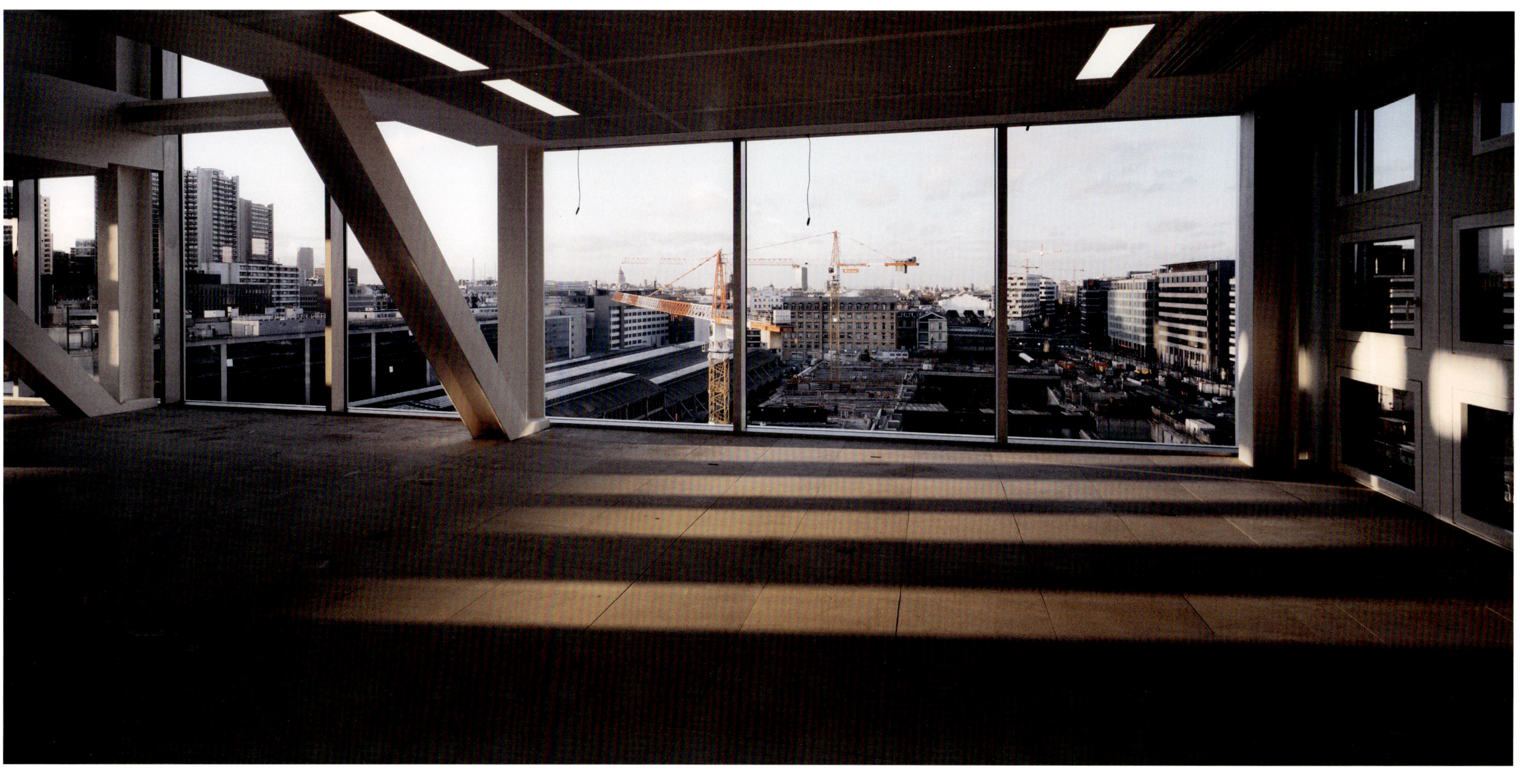

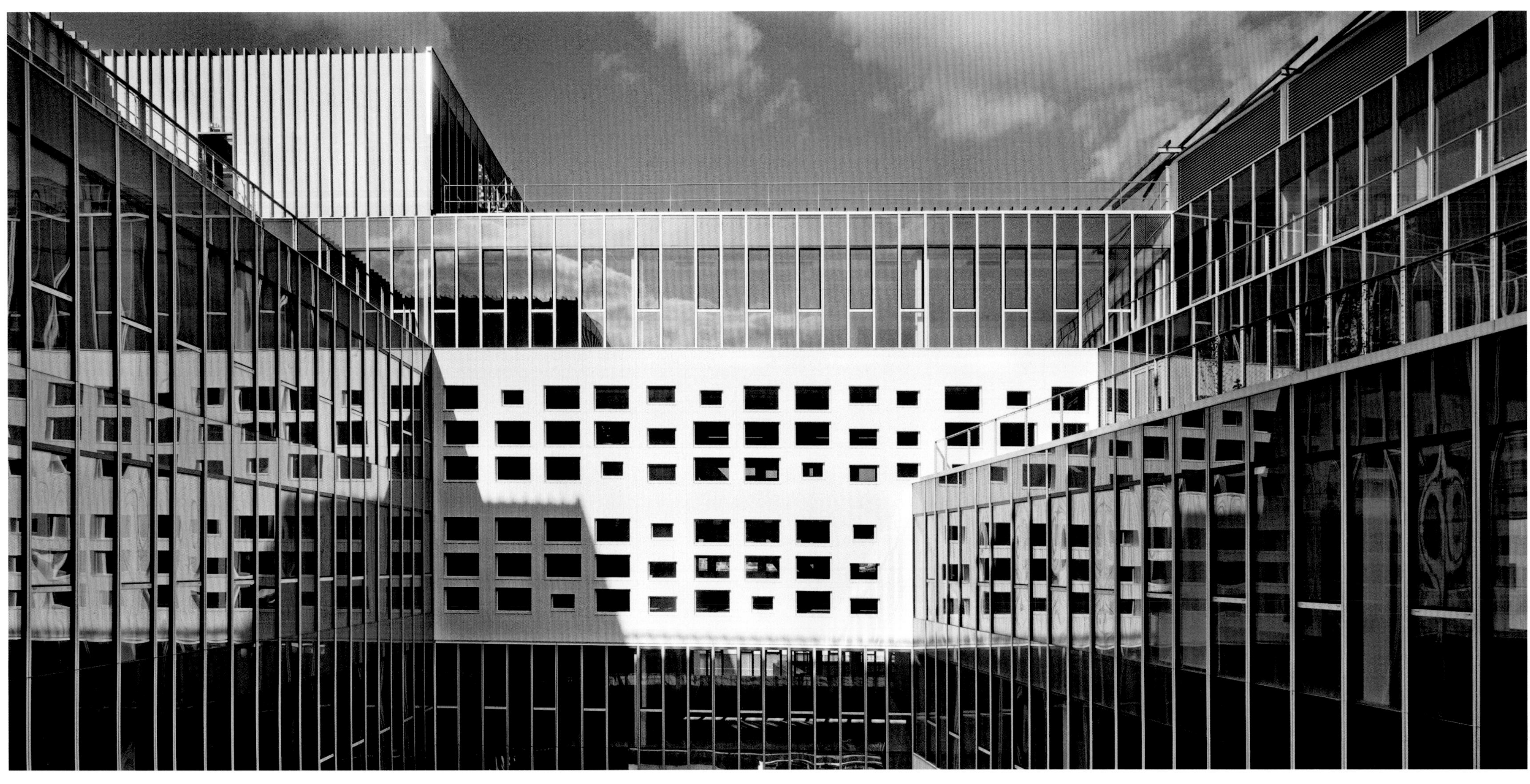

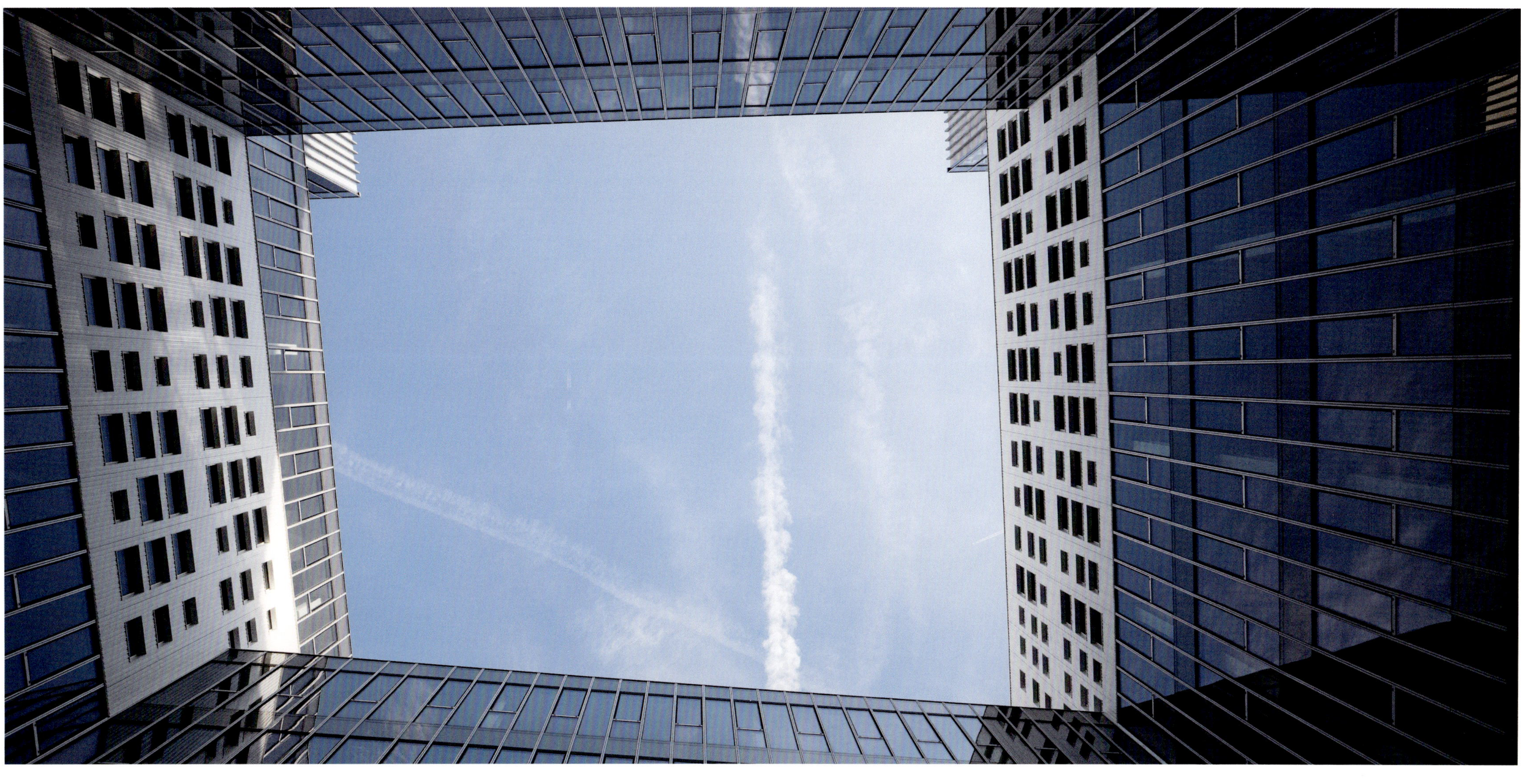

March 2019

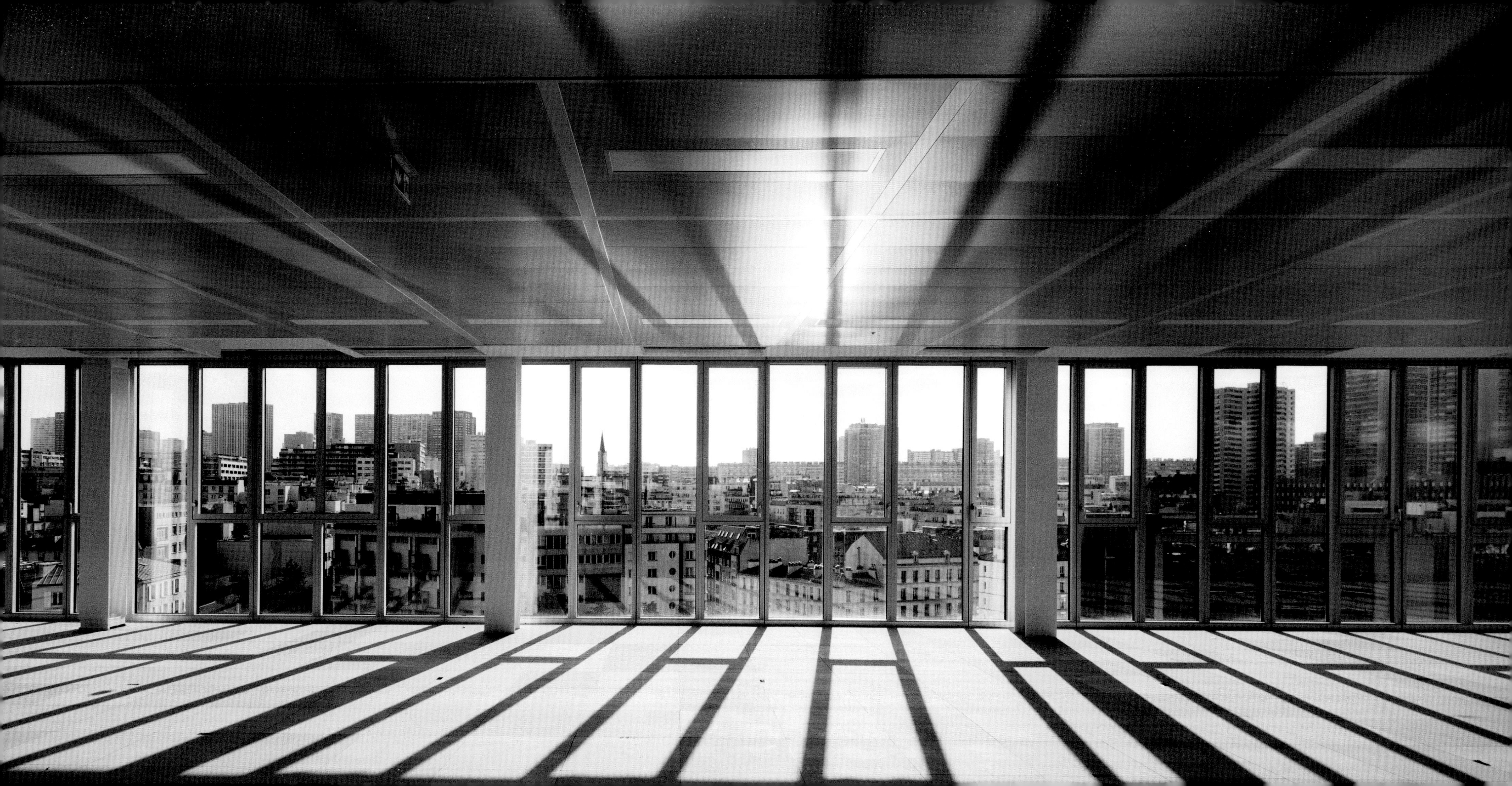

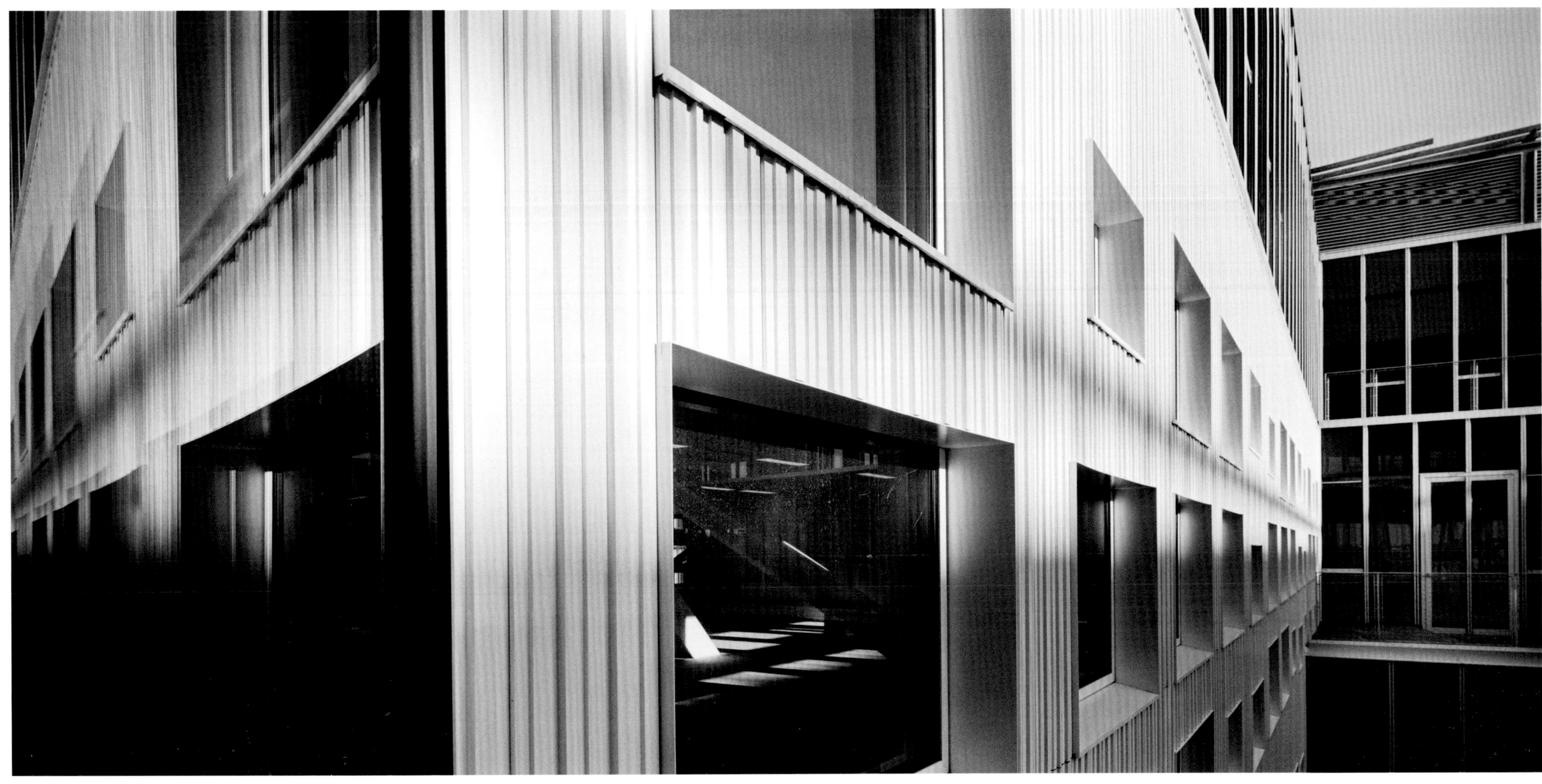

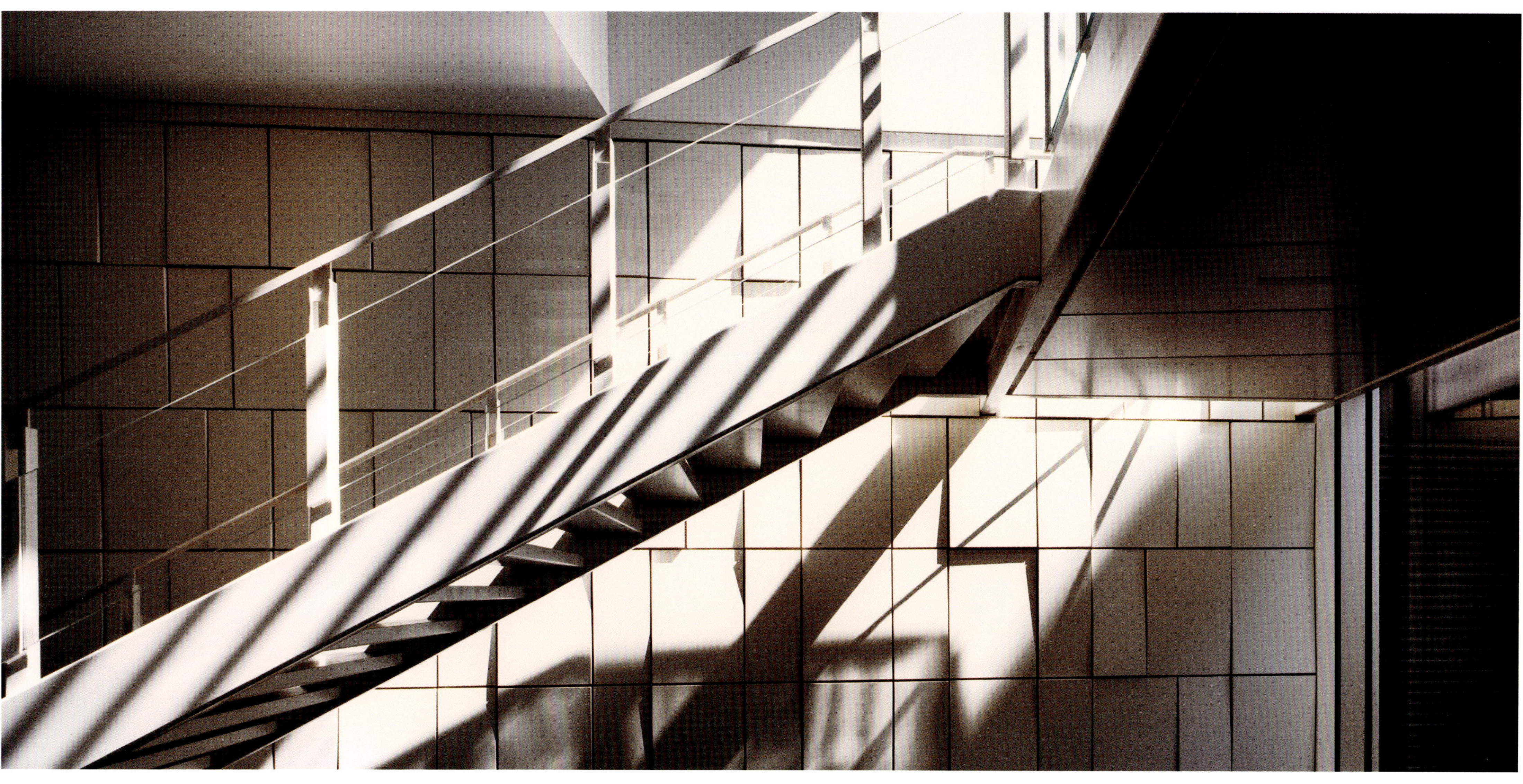

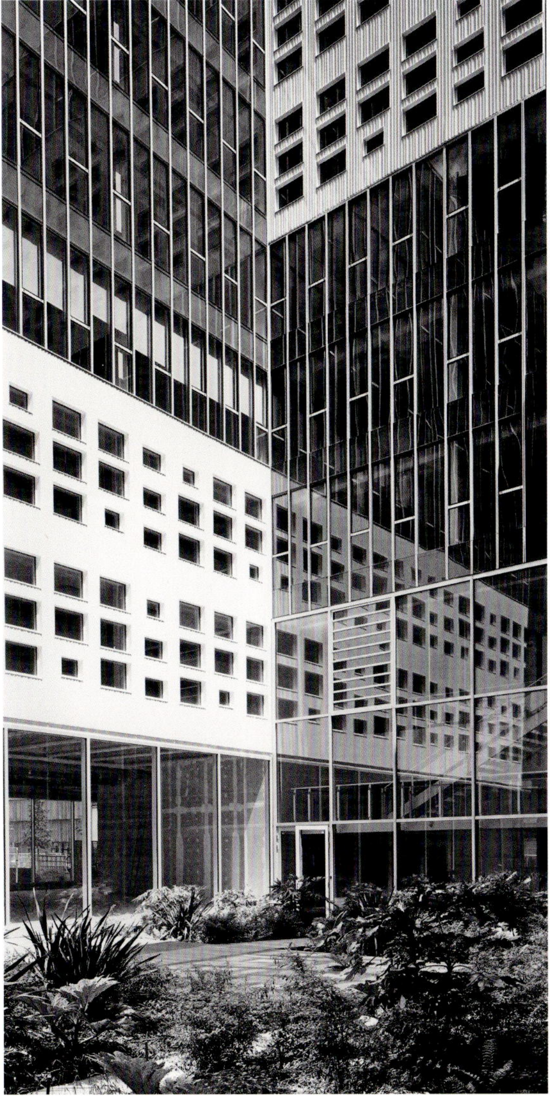

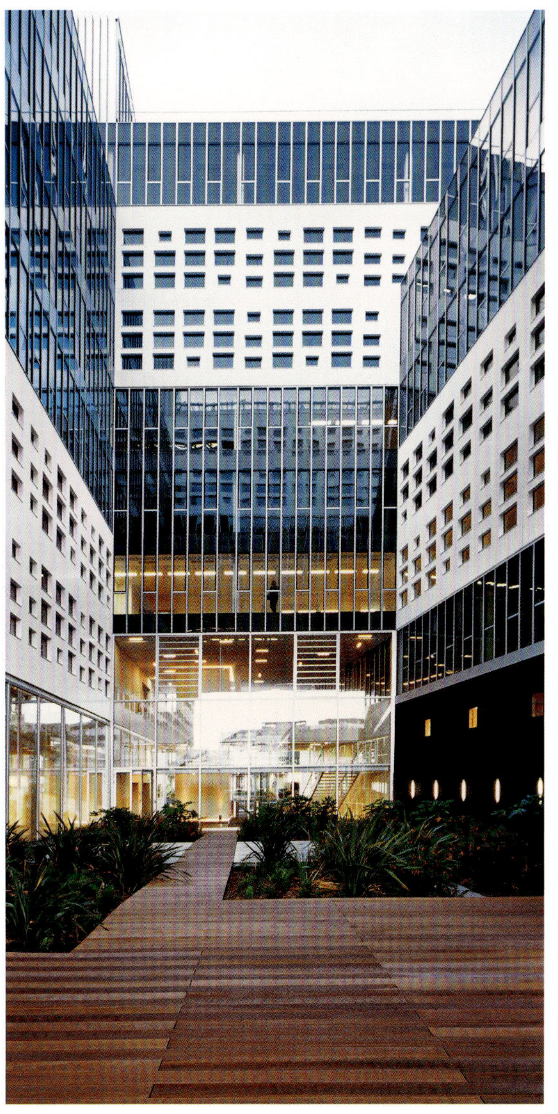

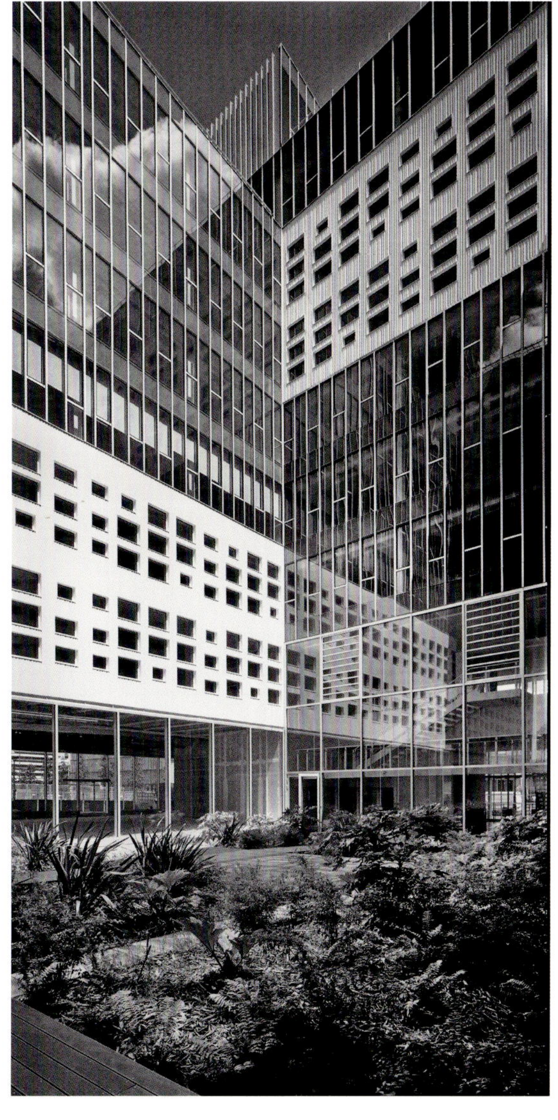

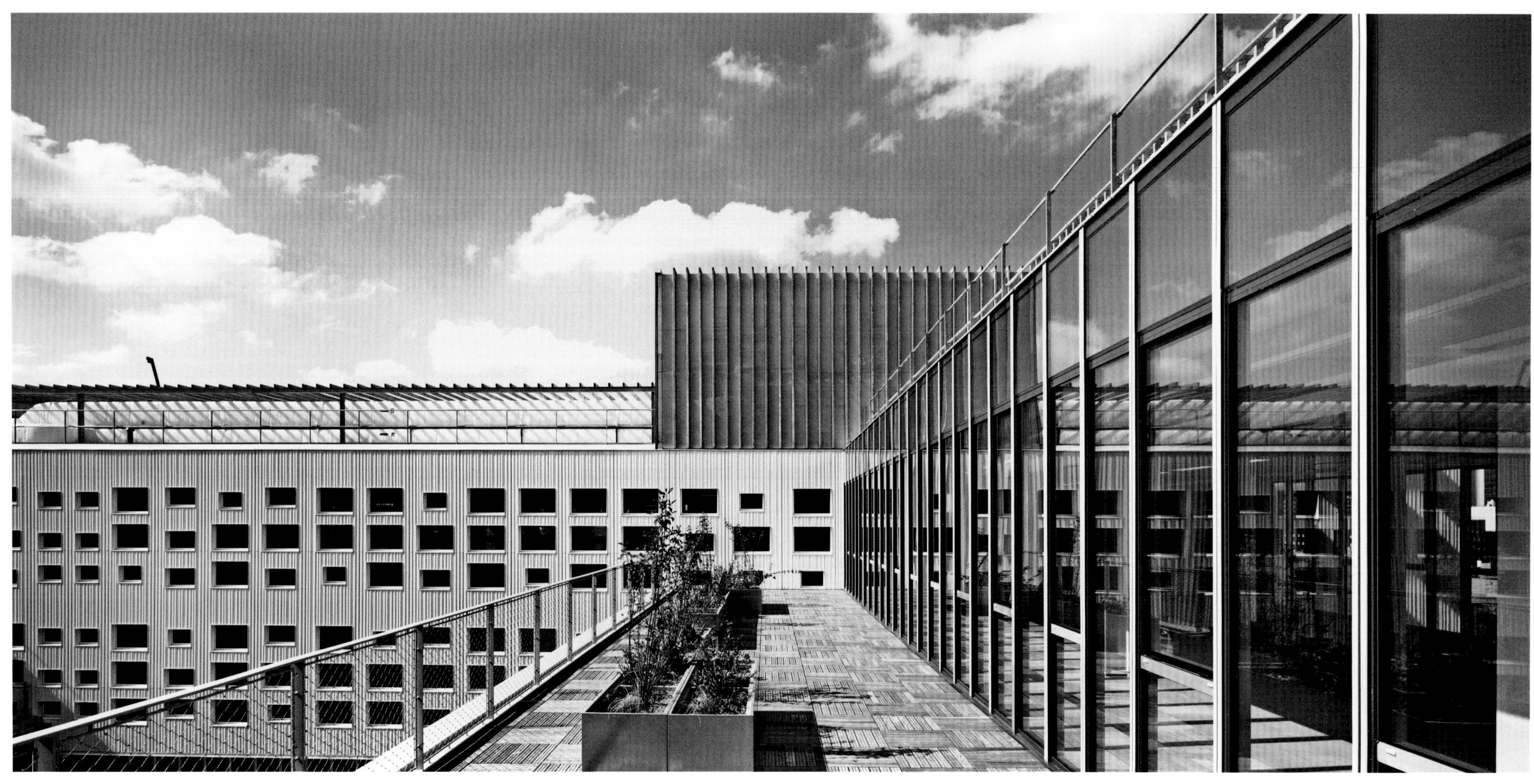

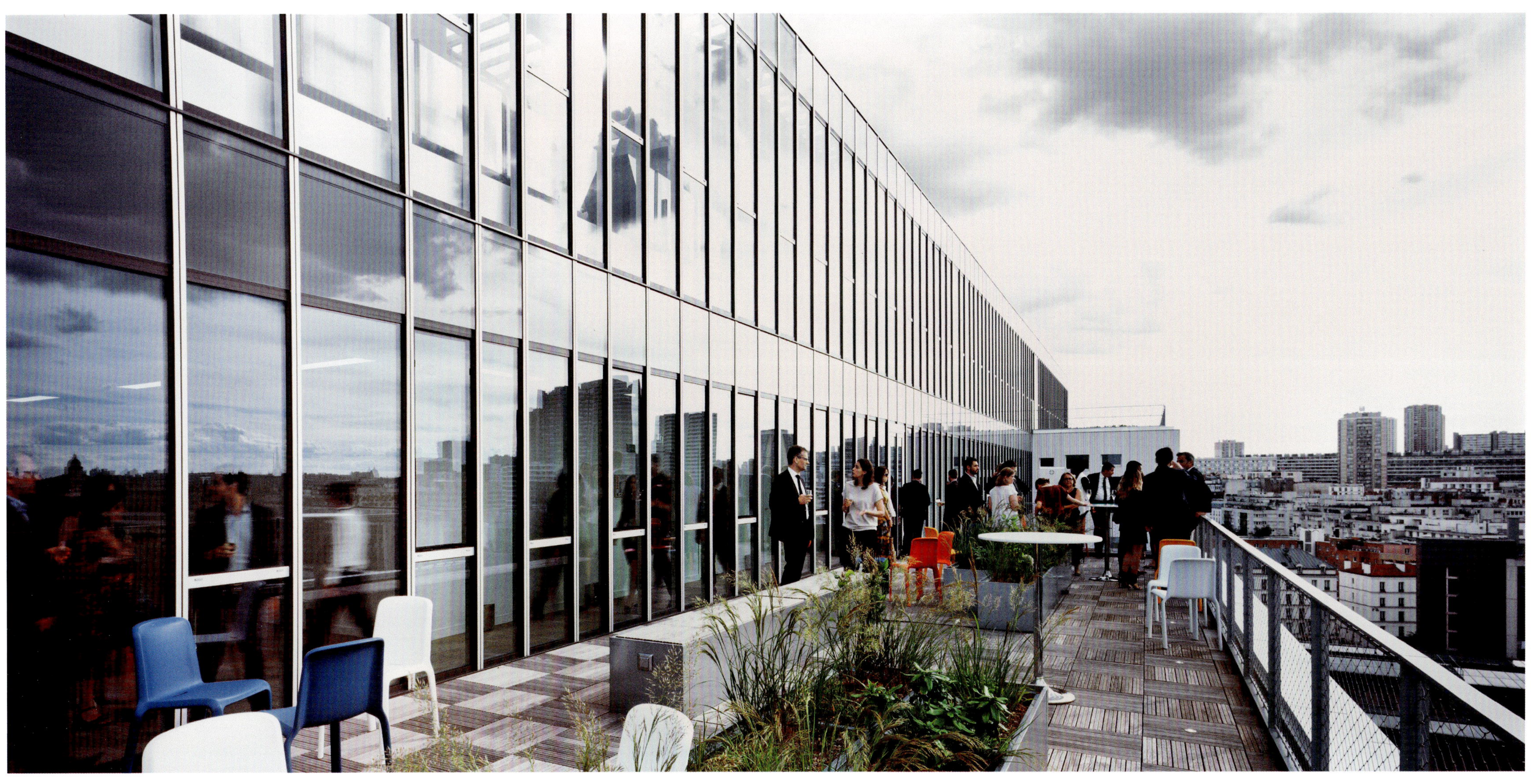

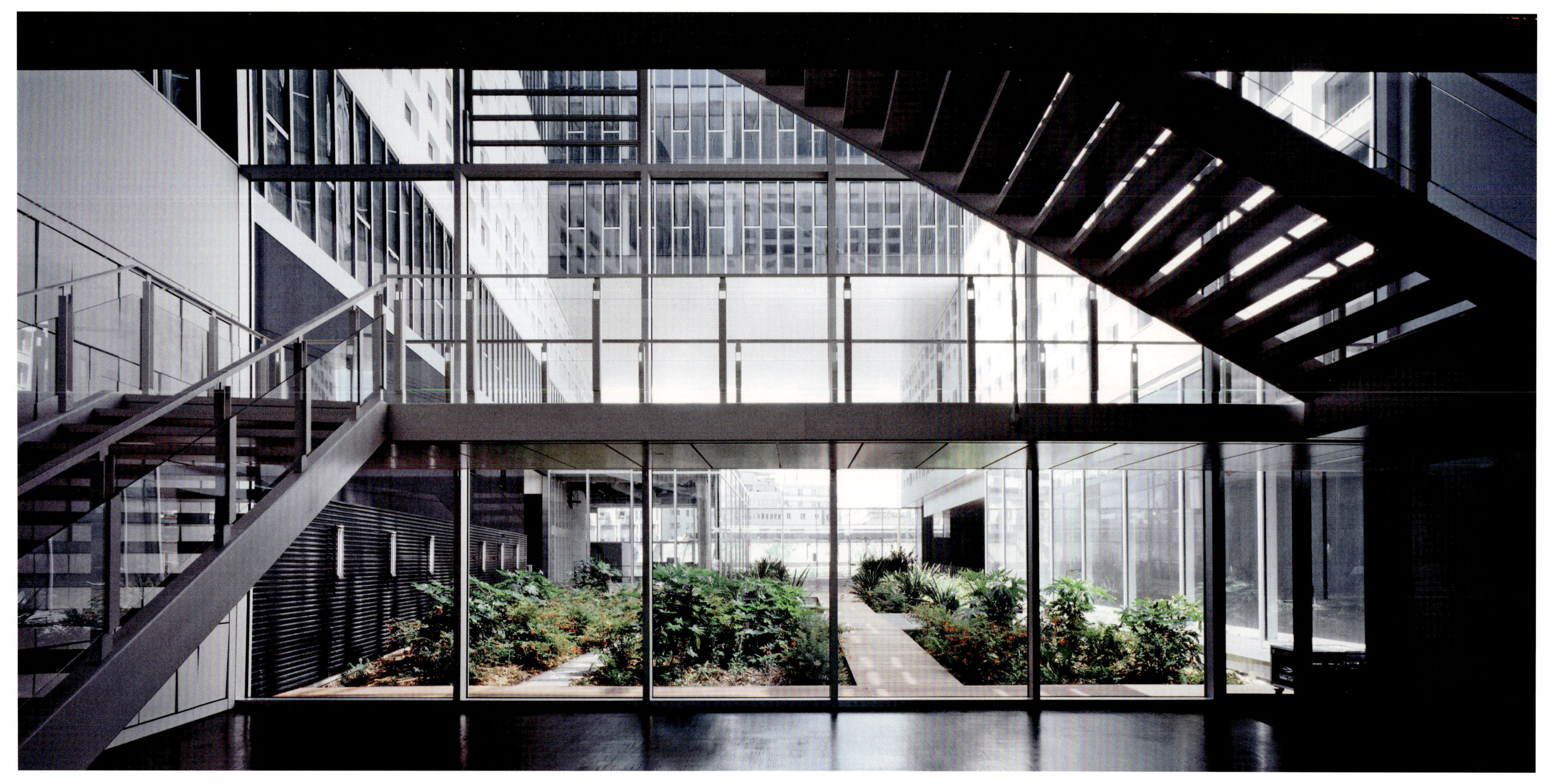

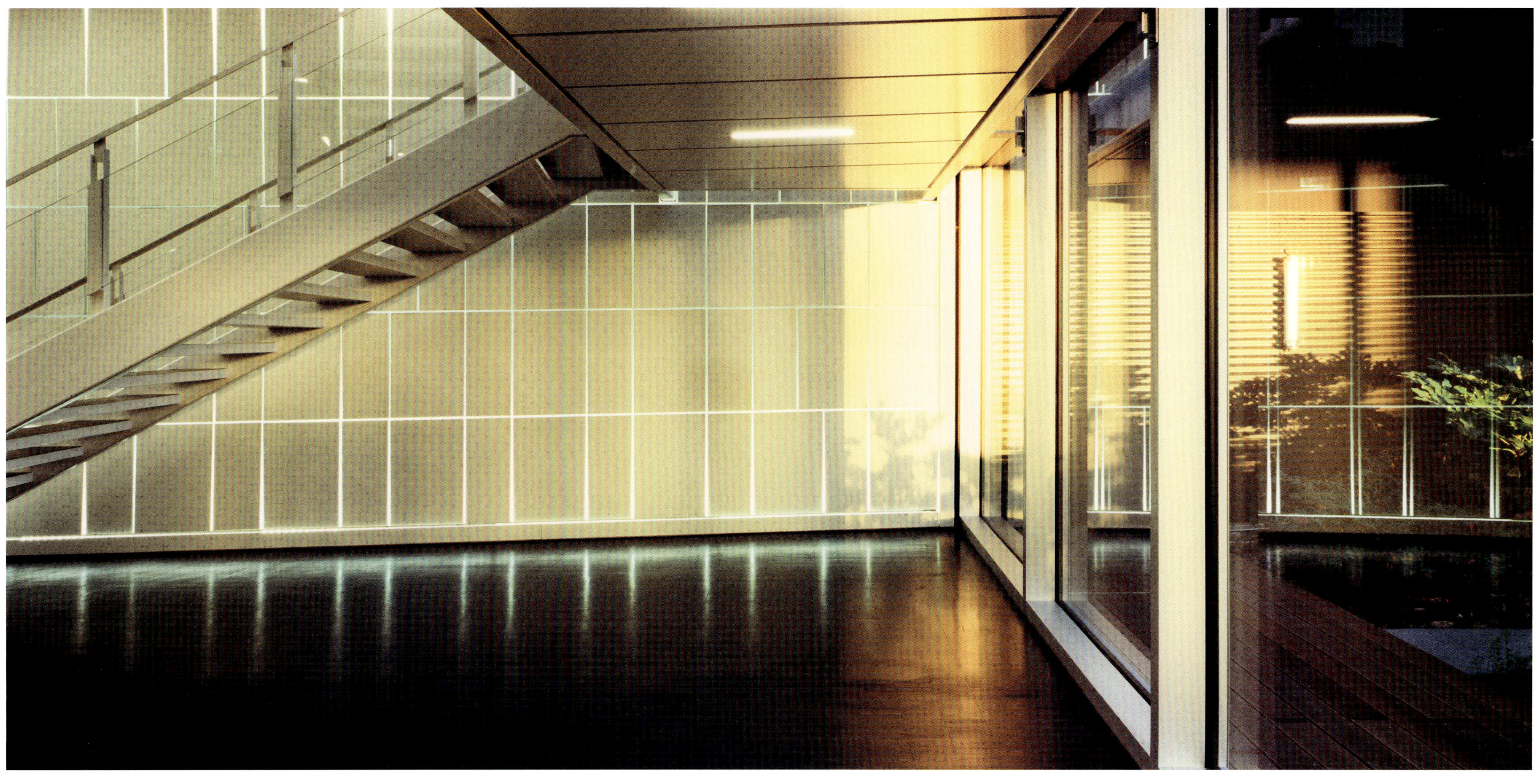

June 2019

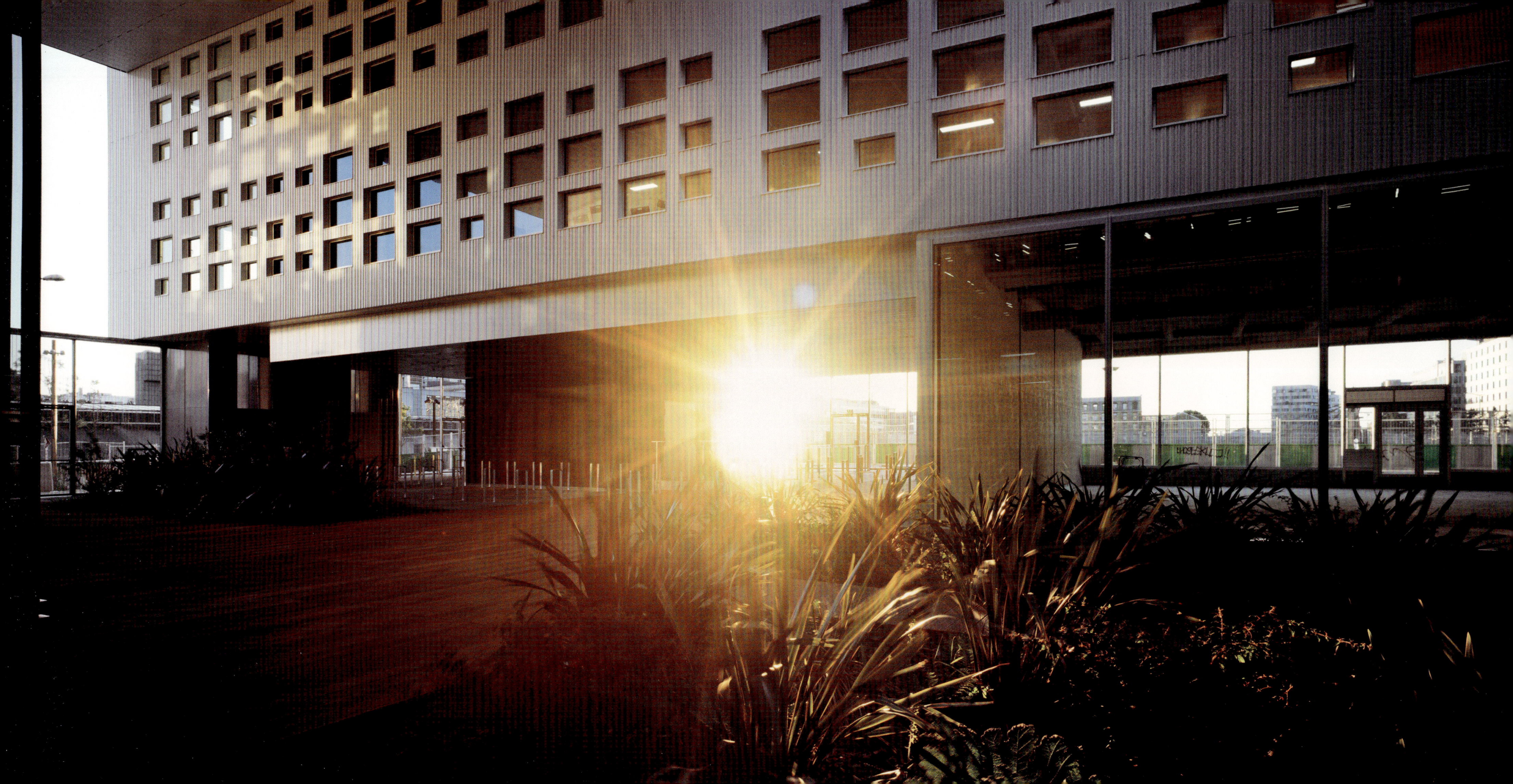

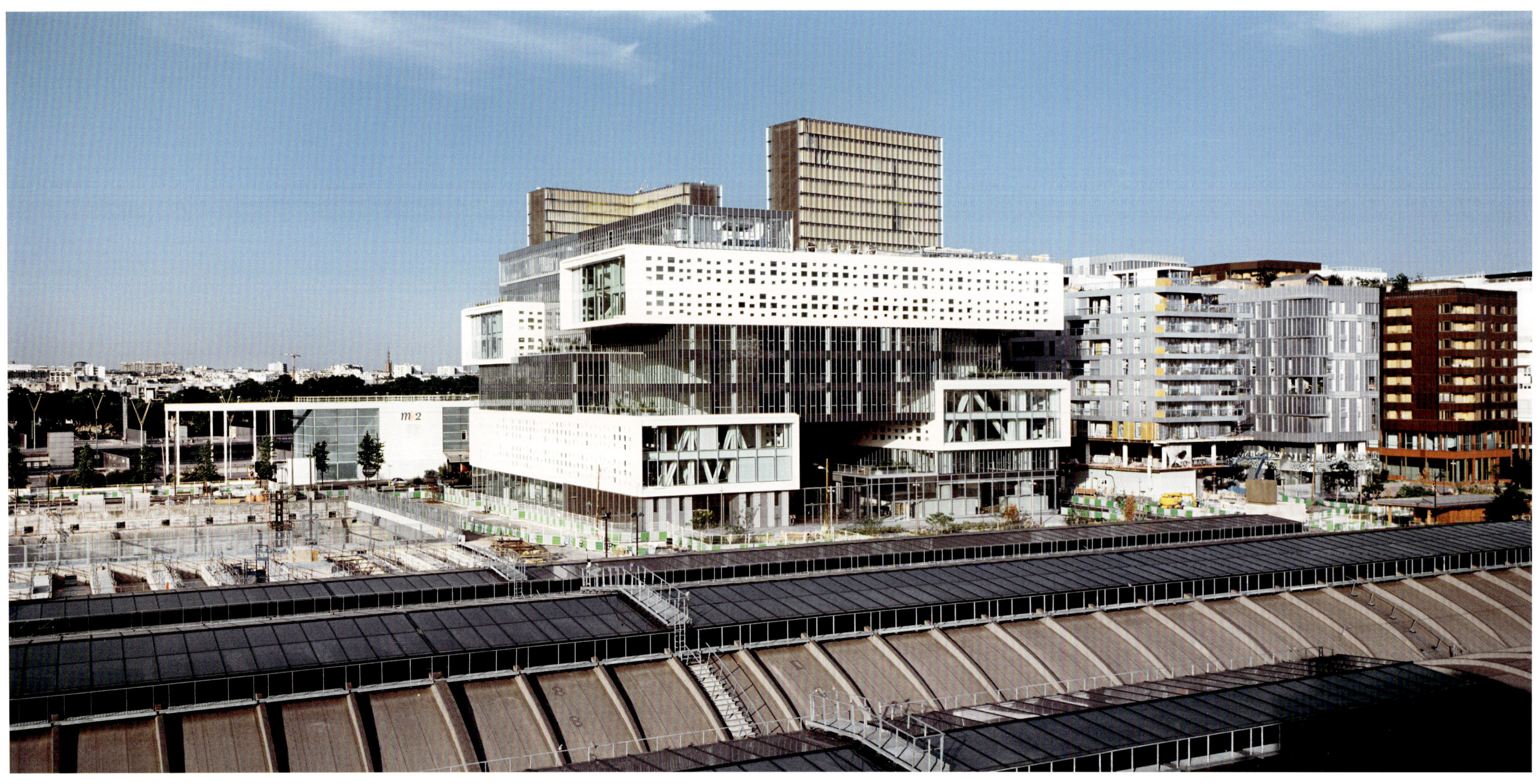

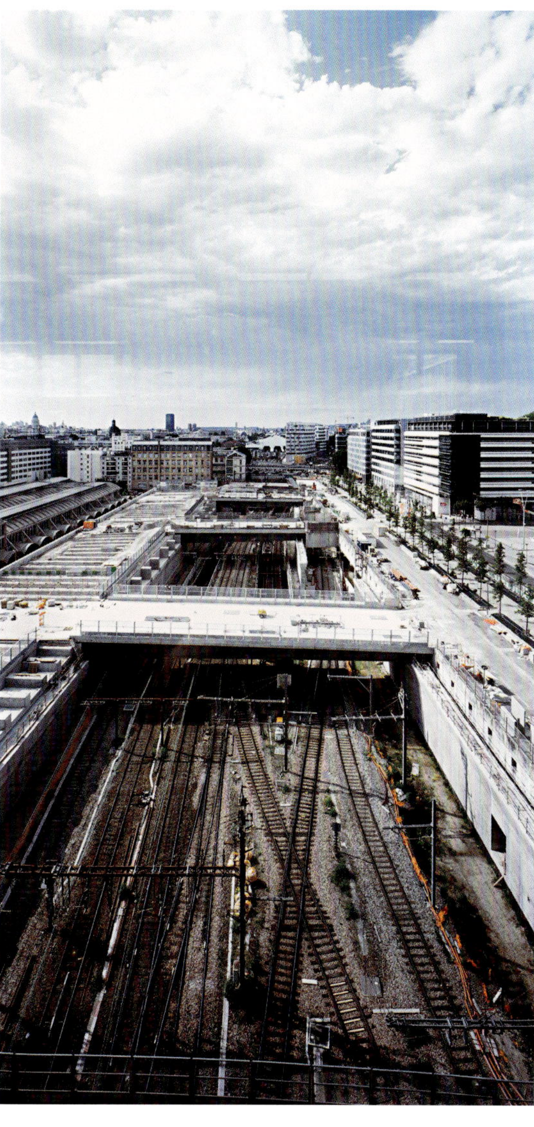

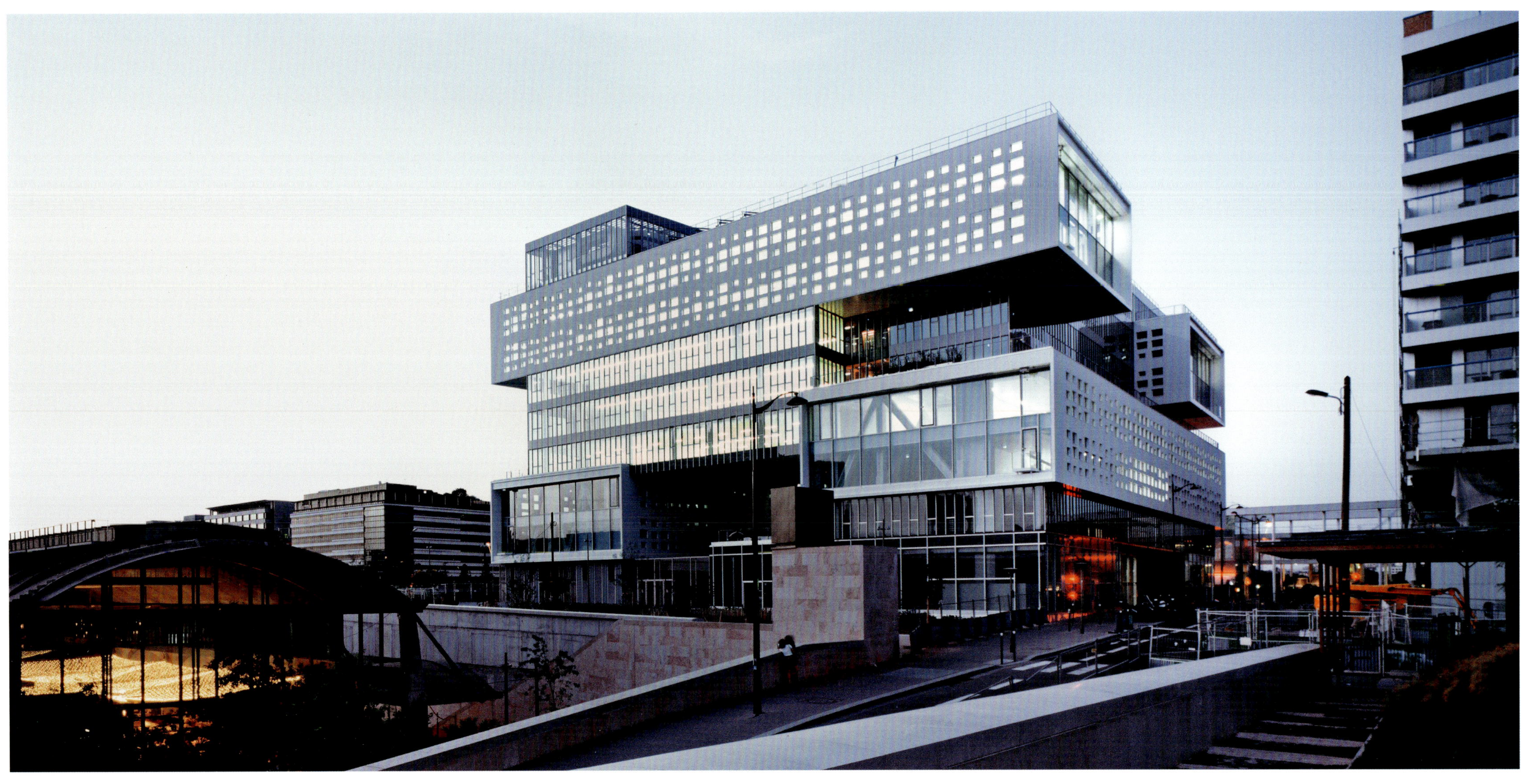

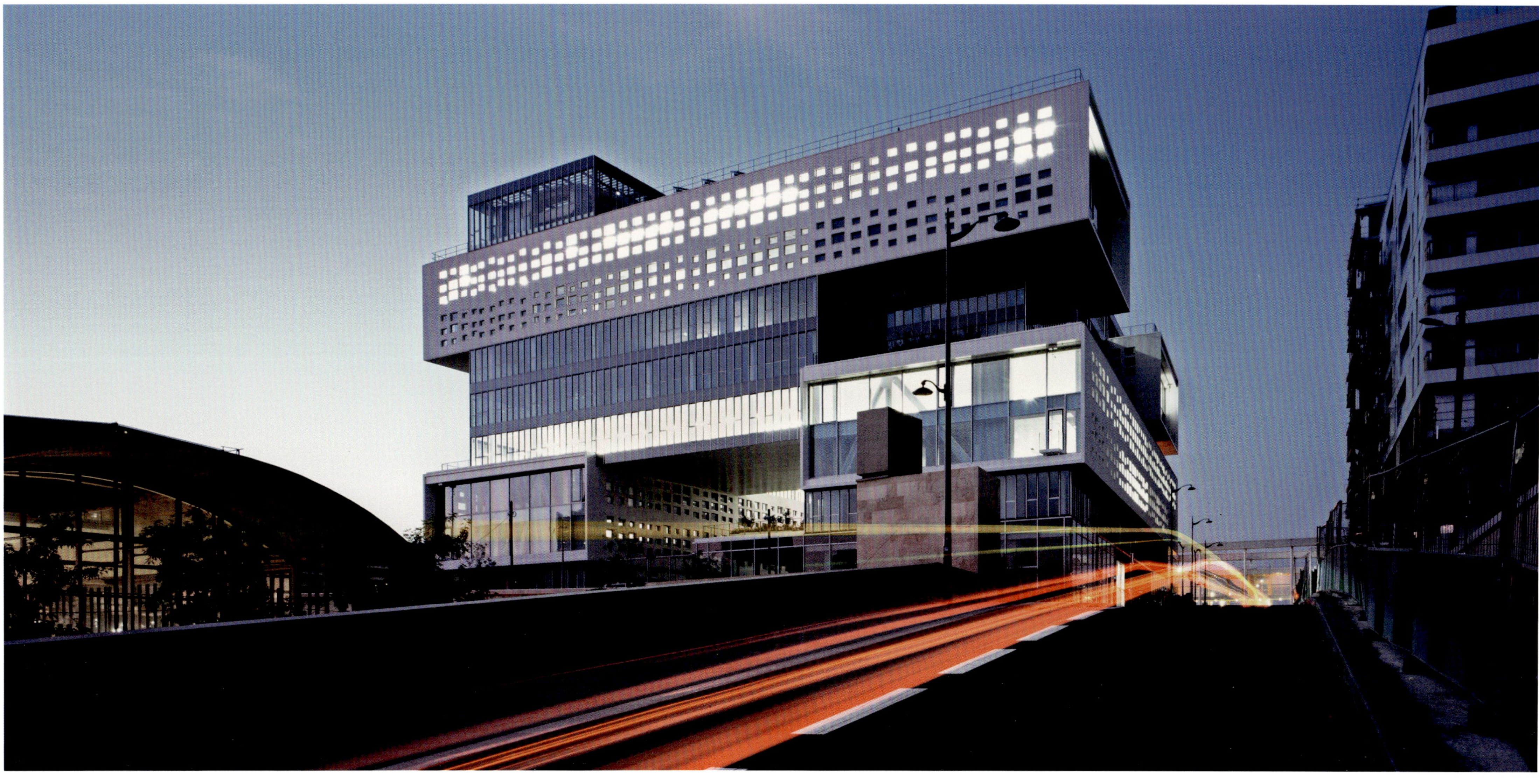

June 2019

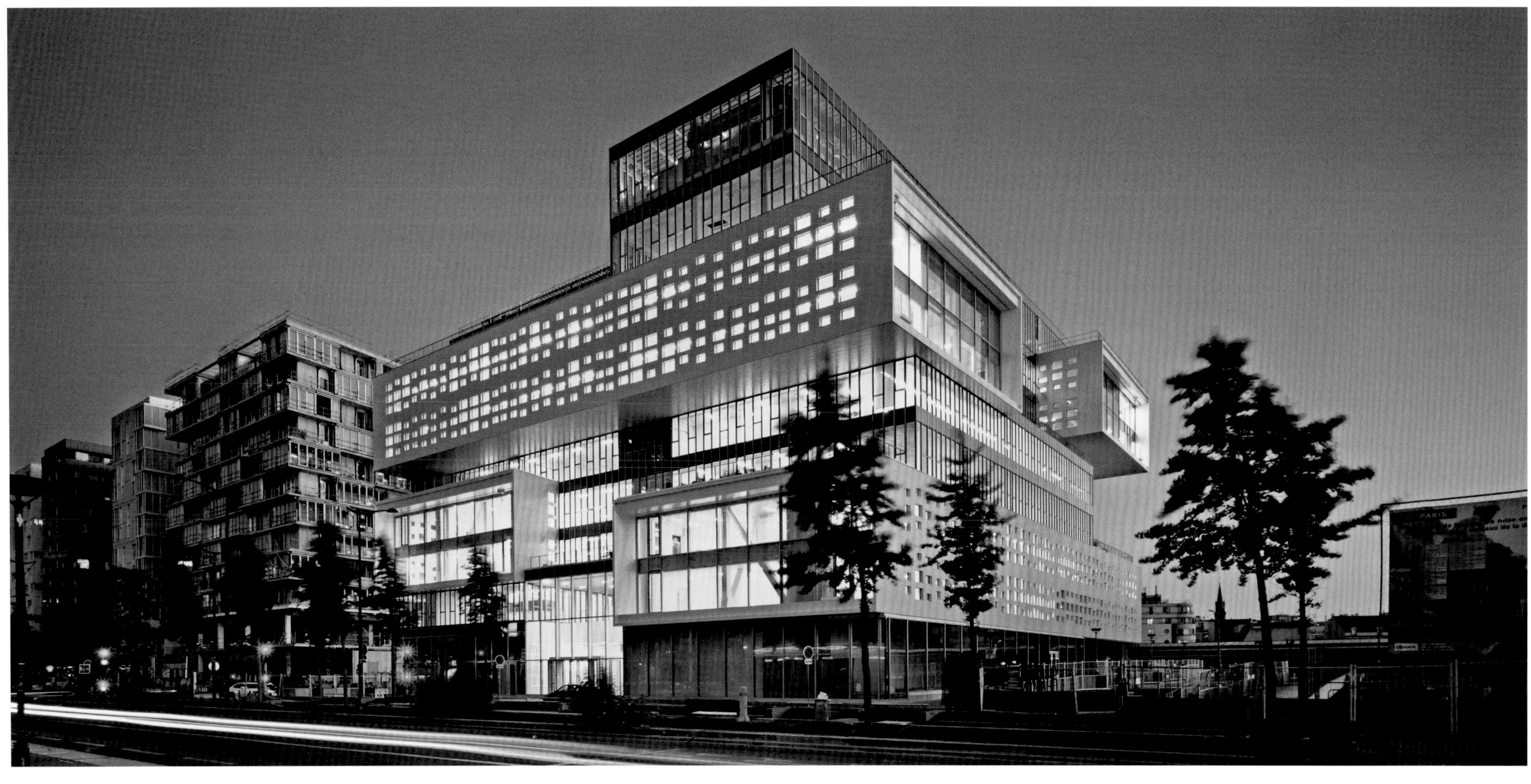

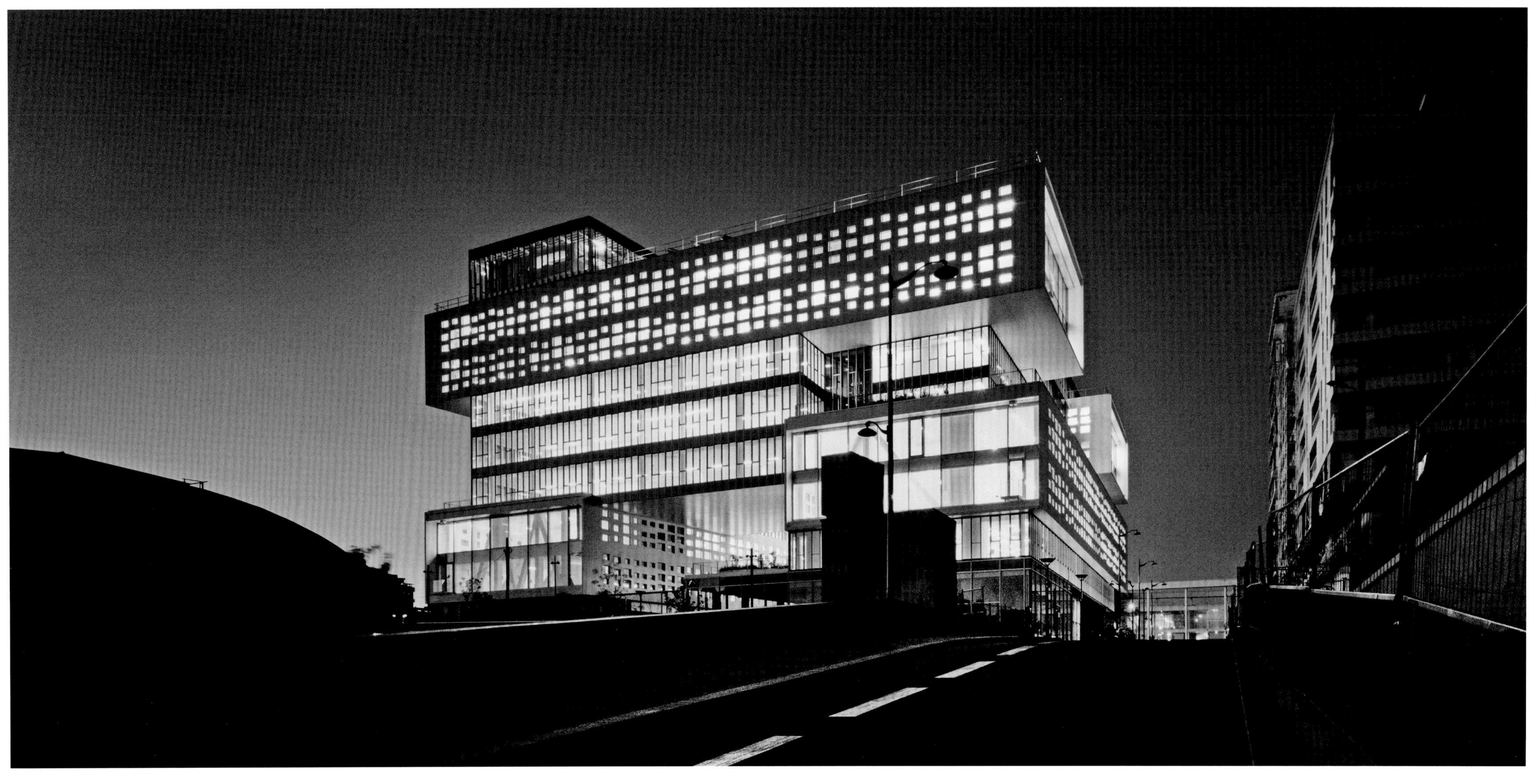

A Conversation

Marc Mimram, Erieta Attali, and Jean Attali

JA Most people are trapped in the world of images. When I say "trapped" I mean that people are used to looking at images, even though the power of photography lies in leading the attention of people to the topic. So when we are speaking of images, photographic images of architecture in particular, we have to stress that the aim should not be to look at the image as such, but rather to look at something through the image, and through somebody else's vision.

MM Yes, there is always a danger, which is to look at the picture itself instead of trying to understand the work through the images. But I want to take this risk because I hope that we will go deeper than the surface of the image; we will advance further.

JA The way we have to see this photographic series is very explicit. I mean that the relationship between two pictures is not the relationship between the two frames, i. e., the continuity of the skyline or a hill. It is very important to attract the attention of the viewer to the vision and not to the artifact of the image. And it starts with what you see; it is not the building as such that is seen, but the relationship of the building to its surroundings.

EA Photography is not about the thing that you look at, but rather the action of looking through. And this is what makes architectural photography both intentional and consequential in the understanding of built space. There are photographers who are attracted to forms, a sort of mannerism of image: they end up photographing architecture in ways that might produce interesting compositions but in the end they are misinterpreting, and misleading. The mere fact that this is possible shows the importance of looking through the image and not at it.

JA Absolutely. I think both picture and architecture are most interesting when working as lenses. And in Airtime it is totally clear that this position of the different terraces and floors manages this looking-through, this vision from inside to outside, from the structure of the building to the surroundings of the city.

EA This building is a device to help you connect with the views and a space to move within; you thereby lose the distinction between inside and outside. I also feel that somehow you are rooted and uprooted at the same time; it creates a multidimensional atmosphere. Of course when the whole railway is covered, there might be no further memory of the people working there and the depth of that open space; but at least this ever-changing process of linkage between the building and the city will be preserved in the photographs.

MM Not only is there a relationship between the building and the landscape as Erieta likes to emphasize, but the whole idea of this structure is that of a device that would give you the opportunity and freedom to see. When I understood this, it was a great moment for me. You might remember when we first talked about it: when you are inside the two white beams the structure frames your understanding of the city; and when you are outside this structure you are completely free. The first thing we did for the competition is to take a balloon and take a picture from every vantage point, to see what the people would see.

EA In the latest series of pictures that we saw with Marc, there are some photographs where the interior space is blending with the outside, almost becoming a cloudscape. You are floating, and perceive the urban context dissolved through this structural environment. It is also very fortunate we photographed it before any of the furniture arrived, because then you have the interior as an extension of the landscape where everything unfolds in an urban scale; this continuum would have been broken had there been furniture in the foreground.

MM This idea of floating is very interesting; I have also wondered: What will people feel being in a building that spans fifty-eight meters? Would they feel like they ware connected to the ground? We are connected to the ground at six points: four in one side and two on the other side. Will this make a difference? I think so. I think you have an instinctive feeling of the space around you wherever you are.

JA I recall the experience of the apartments of Le Corbusier, L'Unité d'Habitation, where the span of the building inside is sixteen meters plus the two balconies, which makes it eighteen meters, and the experience of this length of the apartment means something very important. So when you are speaking of fifty-eight meters it is a way to enlarge the experience of the space enormously.

MM Not only the experience of the space, but also that of gravity. And there is also another element—the domesticity of the working areas—because of the double-height volumes and terraces. The architecture in this case offers you a very different type of experience since the typical office building is, under normal circumstances, eighteen meters wide with a long corridor running parallel to the façade. In our case we have width ranging from nine to eighteen meters, which means we have the capacity to put terraces wherever we want.

JA Could you, Marc, develop this idea of domesticity? Because your building presents a paradox of managing domesticity within an office setting. I think it is very important because the experience of space for everybody begins with the experience of *chez soi*, of being at home. So the root of the spatial experience is that of being at home, with or without comfort. It is the native relationship between our bodies and space; and for me, it is the beginning of architecture. So when you are speaking about domesticity in this office building, it is the most important thing for me.

MM You know Marc-Antoine Laugier's story of how architecture is related to the primitive hut and how many people argue that architecture began there. But what about today's hut? We spend twelve hours per day in our homes—with seven of them sleeping—but we are spending eight hours in the office. So where is your house? Do you know what domesticity in an office is? It is people colonizing the space with their personal things, their lives unfolding into a vibrant chaos: it is the sound of the piano, the scattered books and so on. So this is a kind of domesticity. In this building, Airtime, the relationship between inside and outside will change completely from that of a regular office building. In office buildings you are always inside; in New York you cannot even open a window. But here, not only can you open a window, the window is also related to the terrace and the terrace is huge; I hope that the people will be connected to the terrace, connected to the view, and connected to the world. For me, if they have to work within the world they have to be connected to the world. They cannot be in the stock market, as in Wall Street, in the dark, just concentrated on buying, selling, and dealing. We have to be connected to the world. This is the main enabling power of architecture.

JA This is clear, but this relationship with the world, toward the world, begins or is rooted in this primitive experience of being at home, being located somewhere in the world. The importance of being somewhere related to the others within the limits of a certain space is the true root of the experience of architecture. And you know, in order to open the mind of people toward architecture, it is so important to relate this personal experience to builders. That's why I am terribly interested in the domesticity of the building that you were talking about. I would like to ask Erieta about this topic of domesticity; I know it is a very paradoxical topic, and I would also like to know how you experience it in your practice.

EA Within my daily life I am not exactly connected with the specific routine of a certain space. Rather, every space becomes my home. I never feel unfamiliar with the places I enter: it is a process that I have developed throughout the years, after changing several homes, lines of work, and spaces.

MM Even with the landscapes?

EA Absolutely. Especially after I start photographing: the photographic process allows me to develop a deep connection with places where I find myself for the very first time.

MM But you also photograph houses.

EA Yes, but I have a certain difficulty when entering houses with a lot of personal items. There is a feeling of discomfort and distraction, and this is why I prefer communal spaces; my photographs of public and institutional projects carry my visual language more effectively. The first thing is to know what the context is about, and then to understand the building itself, but it always starts with the context. I walk around the streets, move inside and out, and spend time around buildings—as we did in Morocco, Marc will remember with the bridge. He told me: *"today we have walked twelve kilometers to make five photographs, and then we walked many hours in the morning and some kilometers and at the end we hardly even used those photographs."* But that is my routine to get to understand a site. I also see the photographs collectively: it is not about one picture, but rather a puzzle to be built, a mosaic. I would like to imagine all these images that I made and I visualize them together. There are never single pictures, but several groups of them. And very often in these series of pictures the empty spaces between the pictures themselves are just as important. They build a rhythm of reading and understanding.

JA Speaking of empty spaces or gaps makes me think of the importance of the void, both in the spatial and in the aesthetic sense; but also in your experience with reality. And that sounds very Jewish. The main thing is that God is not there, so it means that we have this interest in the absence for the world that isn't full. There is this presence of the void: a presence of absence. I think that feeds and nourishes Marc's experience of architecture. Would you agree?

MM I am actually very astonished because the void from the point of view of engineering is the most important thing. Robert le Ricolais says "don't put materials but put the voids in the structure." The idea of inertia, which is the most important one in the structure's resistance, is the idea of the void. The most important space I have ever been inside, from the engineering point of view, was Brunelleschi's dome in Florence's Cathedral, Il Duomo, because between the two layers of the curved roof you are in the void. You are within the resistance of the void itself and you are experiencing it, moving inside of it. This was the foundation of my work, of my understanding of engineering. This is the most important experience of the void that I have ever had in my life. That is where the story of the Solférino footbridge began: in the Solférino footbridge you are going from one point to another, through the void. I don't know why I didn't speak about this before; this is the most important thing if you want to understand the way I practice engineering. You are in the void; you are passing through it, like opening a window out to the sky. You have a window between the two arches that connects you to the sky; the idea of gravity is strongly related to the idea of negotiating your relationship with the void. So this is the most important thing: not only the fact that that I have not talked about this until now, but I have also never connected it to the Jewish God before either.

JA I am happy because at the end we reach the most important topic of this conversation.

EA Ideas like this take time to unfold: not only verbally but also through the interaction between language and image, which is the whole point of this collaboration. During my first visits to Airtime I was also fascinated by the structure, and the way that it reframes the context. I think that for Marc, as well as myself, it is important to look at the same time through the structure and within the structure. Because the experience of this "machine for viewing" should not be limited to the act of looking outside, but should also emphasize that feeling of being inside the structure; this is what defines your experience of the city. I also think this is what Marc understands and expresses as "the void."

MM To be honest, architecture is the way of hiding and showing; you see what the architect wants to show and you can either understand or not understand what you see. So you have to choose what to show or not. I am obviously part of this culture of showing. But showing does not necessarily mean exposing the "muscles" or the skeleton of the building; for me what is more important is the urban continuity of Avenue de France. I feel as if it was not necessary to show off, or to hide the structure, but instead to feel the structure, to be related to the landscape. This appears in the first stage of the structure's vocabulary, which makes the reading of the project blurry. The invisible elements are just as important as the visible ones.

JA And for you Erieta, how do you do deal with this topic, that is, how do you feel about revealing qualities of architecture that are not really visible?

EA For me the very character of photography is to reveal qualities that are not visible at first, but rather have to be searched for. Of course you can arrive in front of a building and be happy with what you see on the surface. If, however, you research further, especially if you visit an actual, complex site, you will start seeing things that our visual culture has difficulty capturing. There are so many layers, which will often demand a narrative approach through a series of photographs in dialogue; a couple of visually striking but isolated images cannot capture the complexity of diurnal, seasonal, even social transitions. My mission is to look for these things, which we are not trained to see. This is why I spend a lot of hours, even days, on site: it is the only way to become receptive to the nuances of the interaction between a building and its environment, both physical and human. The building unfolds with time. Every component falls into place, as long as you take the necessary time to understand all the unseen interactions that make up architecture.

MM Erieta, when you see something hidden, do you push on it or do you leave it as is?

EA Of course I push: What is the point of leaving it hidden? I show it as my goal. Anyone looking at a picture can interpret in his or her own way, you can never escape the subjectivity; but intention, conscious, and focused intention makes a difference that is communicable through the image. This is why I always try to go beyond documentation.

JA There is also this element of time as a dimension of architecture. For me it is very important to record, as you did, the different stages of construction. Because the construction site is the main square for the architectural narrative: you understand how the building is made. And I think that after the end of the construction you keep in mind the story of construction, which can be either visible or hidden; the architecture somehow narrates the story of the building.

MM The construction is not a phase: the construction is the building. What I notice usually when browsing architectural photos is that you do not see people. I am very interested in seeing people walking because the building is built on "sweat and tears." I want the public to understand that. The building is the memory of that time: the project is, above all, a process. There are two dimensions to this: material and human. The first one is to show what you will not see anymore, like the uncovered railways and exposed structural members. Even if you perceive these elements in the finished architecture, you won't see them in the same way. The second dimension is the idea of the memory of the building through the people that built it up. This memory is what ultimately ties the building to the Earth, since we are a part of that larger environment. A building does not materialize instantly. And I want to understand and communicate the process of that happening. This is why I am very interested in the pictures of Erieta's; they show heaviness, a lot of structure, a lot of steel, a lot of people working in there. These disappearing components of the building, which nevertheless define its final identity, are expressed in the image; I am happy that she could take these photographs.

EA Even for myself, reexamining the first photographs now after two years, I feel this vindication and sense of accomplishment. I am so happy that we have done it. It is a confirmation of how important it is to be present, to enmesh yourself with the project and follow all the small changes and transitions of the structure. I would visit the site at least once every two months. When I was photographing Airtime I always tried to keep in mind the idea of the bridge; but then Marc said that the bridge would not be important because it will be covered. Since that point I decided to really try and show that; not only to show it once, but to try and capture it systematically through the development of the structure and how it reframes and reshapes the landscapes around it. This is, in a way, Marc's own history and heritage: the site throughout its whole process of development before it is totally covered, and the area before the bridge becomes "false ground." By necessity I have to understand Marc's vision through my own language. So, while the structure rises up, I really cannot avoid seeing a bridge there, the workers on it and all the trains speeding under it. This is something that you will not experience in two years or so, but that is nevertheless part of the building's identity.

JA I hear something else here, which has sociopolitical overtones. If the value and the wealth rest on the work as such, it means that you have a deep investment against the devaluation of the work. These days physical labor is much devalued, so you are reminding us that the reality of (labor) value rests on the work. Would you say this is important to you?

MM Yes, don't forget that my father was a tailor. I can remember as a child seeing people looking at the fabrics, cutting the material, and tracing the patterns. When you apply the pattern on the fabric you do it in such a way that you do not lose too much fabric when cutting. My father would come to me and say, "Marc this shoulder is not well done." Everything was important: material, the labor that shapes it, the process that avoids waste through efficiency. In the end, this is what we do now with steel: from the details to the whole, because the materials connect the two. When I greet somebody and ask them how they are, I instinctively focus on the fabrics that they wear, like my father used to do. He was touching things to see how they behaved, just to understand if it was silk or wool or some other fiber. Engaging with materiality like this was important.

EA I remember we were on a trip in Tokyo with Marc, entering different places, like boutiques and clothes stores. He would start touching things, and not only the displayed items, but also the walls and surfaces; he would scan everything with his gaze trying to understand materials and shapes. It was very interesting for me to witness that first hand, and get an insight into how he approaches architecture.

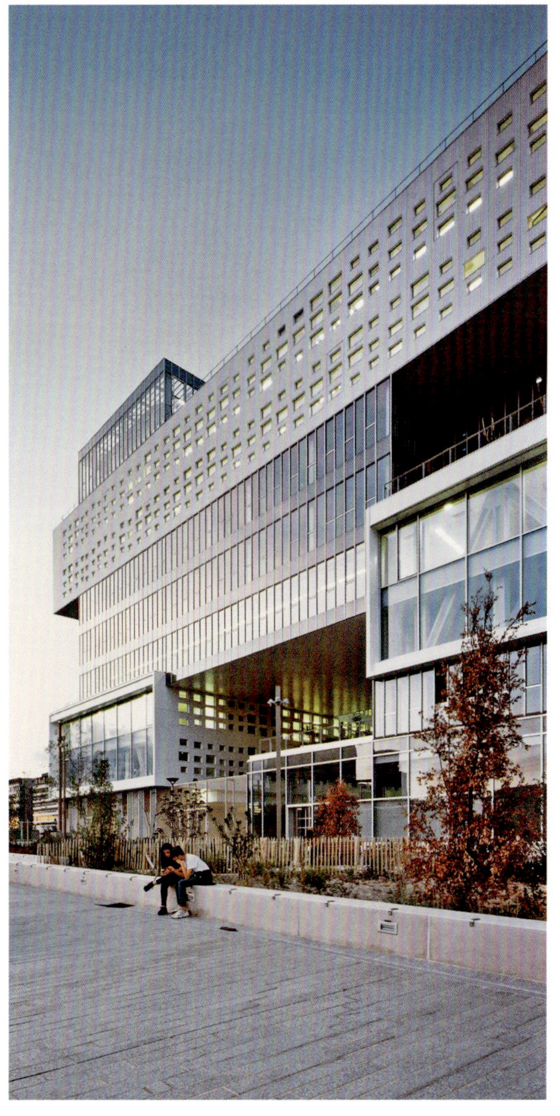

MM But my hands are part of my eyes also.

JA Erieta, you are also visually involved with texture.

EA Yes, part of my work as an archaeological photographer was to reveal textures. It was an essential process, connected to the proper scientific identification and documentation of the findings. I was especially fixated on wall paintings: ancient walls and architectural surfaces in tombs, as well as micro-sculptures and ivory objects found underground. I would try to reveal all the textures and the shapes of these tiny artifacts, and it was not easy. Often I would receive a trolley with maybe two hundred of them, having to reveal them one by one. This way of work has carried over to my architectural photography: the revealing of textures.

MM How did you pass from the small archaeological scale to landscapes?

EA Archaeological fragments are effectively remains of daily objects and buildings, scattered within the site but strongly related to one another. It is part of the archaeological process to try and understand the complete image that these remains describe, and you do that by revealing their relation to the context. Therefore, my work started involving entire archaeological sites where the connecting tissue between eroded fragments of architecture was the landscape itself. So I had to photograph the landscape as well; it was inescapable. I remember one of my most important commissions covering a whole excavation site: it was in Knossos, Crete. It has special importance to me because of the timing as well. It took place immediately after my first five-month stay in Japan, where I covered contemporary glass architecture throughout the country. From glass in a very avant-garde setting to a more than three-thousand-year-old stone palace, the contrast was very intriguing and challenged my whole conceptual toolset as a photographer. Both were landscapes with fragments of architecture, but in radically different manifestations.

MM Obviously archaeology speaks to memory, but you are talking about memory also through your contemporary work?

EA Yes, memory operates on different scales, and that is also something that I first glimpsed through Japan and Knossos twenty years ago. I found myself switching from almost abstract glass architecture set within Japanese landscapes, back to an active archaeological site where I meticulously photographed wall-by-wall, millimeter-by-millimeter, every little trace with scientific precision. These were two very different ways to approach human-made structures and to consider the memories encoded in them. On the one hand you have glass layers whose reflections compress landscape and architecture into one; they fold them together and create this narrative of intermeshed content and context. On the other hand there are literal material layers, solidified one upon another after centuries of being underground; an archaeological narrative, almost a journal of these transitions, is written within the textures of the crusted walls.

MM That's the point. There is memory in the archaeology, and you began with that, but maybe you are more interested in memory in contemporary architecture because you have done past work with the eyes of archaeology.

EA Perhaps, but memory is an inseparable part of the experience of architecture, regardless of its time period. When photographing a glass pavilion by Kengo Kuma and Associates in New Canaan, Connecticut, I did so in the span of two years and throughout the seasons. The transition of seasons, and the way this impacts the experience of the space, is tied to the idea that space is continually inscribing memories on itself through interaction with the context. Space is a layered experience: it amounts to much more than the exterior appearance of a building, or its image. There is a fragile balance between the structure, the natural environment, and light and weather phenomena—always shifting.

MM Fragility, this is it: the fragility that you perceive when looking at the Earth, at the landscapes. That's what I am trying to do: negotiate this fragile balance. And there is this one word that I never use, but it keeps coming back to me, and that is "integration." A lot of people ask me whether I could or would integrate my project into the landscape. I always reply: How can you integrate a bridge in the middle of a valley? Imagine spanning a bridge, from hillside to hillside: we are dealing with an act of violence towards the landscape and the most we can aspire to is to try to and create a dialogue with the landscape. It is a balancing act. Erieta understands this, so she is taking the ephemerality of the landscape as a starting point and explores the interface with the constructs, with architecture and its image. And speaking of image, think this also relates to the idea of architectural style. Style has no meaning at all if it's disconnected from all the topics that we were talking about before; architecture is not a fashion product.

JA But I think style is not a useful word; what is more important is the manner in which you are giving form. I would like to know if Erieta, when she makes these kinds of pictures, is taking care of this expression of the architecture, of the particular form.

EA The building speaks for itself; it actually directs the photographic session in a way. Form is a very important factor in revealing some qualities of the architecture, but so are the atmospheric light conditions that are often tied to a specific geography. I usually try to emphasize certain aspects of a specific building in order to reveal realities that hold true for most architectural works; it is a thought process that moves from the particular to the universal. But of course this does not always work for everyone. For Marc's architecture it is very well defined: in many of his buildings sunshine is very important while for others, such as Airtime, cloudy weather draws the emphasis towards the context, it reveals these connections.

JA Then I have a question about how you feel your own photos; I see first the reaction of materials, surfaces, and the movement of light through reflection. Something in the architecture echoes the way the light is caught; so what is the connection between this reflection of light and the way you enter visually into the building and discover the interior?

EA Each particular work of architecture requires a specific kind of light in order to reveal its intrinsic characteristics; this depends on the form and material, but especially on the context. For example, at Roland-Garros we need sun, otherwise we will get a totally different reading of the place that may reveal other aspects but not the main ones. My understanding is that Marc conceived it, perhaps unconsciously, as a building to be experienced in bright sunlight. When I start observing the site, I know what kind of light would be ideal, but sometimes I have no choice, luckily I had a choice. Most importantly, with Marc's work we always have the choice thanks to this long-form collaboration that we have built. With few exceptions, we can revisit and rethink the work together. In some cases, like Morocco, on the other hand, we did not have a choice; but we were lucky to have the light that we needed. So again, you can see that more than the form, I have to try and follow the light. As a photographer, light gives me the tools to engage with the architectural design, its consequences and intention; form is almost an afterthought.

MM Yes, this is a hard topic. After all, for architecture, form is its most important, its most objective quality. But form is like love; you cannot speak about the thing itself, since it is the result of the whole process that we have been talking about. It is born of the play between materiality, memory, and the landscape. All these are continually talking to us, and we have to listen. The site is something very important, that's why I am saying to the students: "you have to listen to the place, you have to feel the situation which you produce through your design." You make a project in order to begin the dialogue, evolving it as the dialogue unfolds. And a dialogue is a flat process: non-hierarchical but reciprocal and continuous. It is almost the opposite of analysis, which is a top-down approach. I never use that word, by the way. When I was a student we used to have to do an analysis of the site in order to develop a project; this has no sense at all to me, it is irrelevant. There is no sense in analysis in architecture; the project is an analysis itself. The project in a way will react to a situation and will express this reaction in built form. This is what we should be talking about when we are talking about style, or form. And Erieta understands this, the continuous process of dialogue that is very different to top-down analysis.

JA And this lies at the core of this collaboration, between the architect and the photographer: this is the main purpose of this publication and its format.

EA Exactly. I would like to emphasize Marc's contribution, because by giving me the space to operate on my own terms, he has allowed this to happen. This project would not have been possible without Marc allowing himself to explore some new ways of engaging both architecture and landscape. It is worth noting how this collaboration started; what Marc saw in my photographic work, what got him inspired to want to get into this project. I saw the connection from the very start, when attending one of his lectures. But interestingly this project hinged on his decision and not mine. It was fascinating because for an architect or engineer to realize the potential of such a collaboration means that his thought process operates outside the usual strict, technical approach. Architects usually want to hire a photographer for very rational documentation purposes, and there is no potential in that. Marc was gradually, stage by stage, letting me do what I wanted to do; the more he was seeing, the more he was discovering things about himself and his architecture that he was interested in seeing further developed. Our collaboration was even a sort of abstracted dialogue, about the internal dialogues in both architecture and photography: one step ahead, two steps ahead, backwards, forward, in order to unfold all these different stories. So it was not straightforward and it happened within a period of time. Seeing the results gradually, he would process it, work on it; not simply responding to these photos but letting the ideas mature in him. It took some time, of course. I may be very experienced in terms of the visual language of photography, knowing what am I looking for and how to articulate it, but Marc, being an engineer, uses a different vocabulary and different intellectual tools to engage with space. So we needed to perform a sort of visual translation, but we did, and then the real dialogue began.

MM During my first contact with Erieta's photography—and of course after talking about it with her because we are not trained to see intentionality in a photograph: we usually only see the shapes or image—I was very intrigued by two ideas: materiality and limits. Erieta's work hinges heavily on the idea that texture can visually communicate a material reality; then the photograph itself depending on the print medium can layer a second level of texture onto the image, which affects the way we engage with it. And Erieta is using this to perform a transformation of the image of the construction into an act of conversation: of the construction with everything else, including the viewer of the photograph. Engaging with materiality is a way of giving meaning to the Earth's transformation. Architecture, I have said already, is an art of transformation, of taking the world, transforming the world into materials, materials into construction, and construction into new materiality. The relationship that we have with the planet is very central in my conception of architecture; and Erieta's pictures are always referring to that point. The way you read the landscape defines the way in which you read the transformation of the Earth. Then, very closely linked with what we just said is the idea of the limit: the limits between things and how photography can emphasize, diminish, or blend them. I am fascinated by the idea that this is not only a game of words: working with the limit, at the limit, is also the essence of my role as an engineer. I am trying to find out the limit of the weight, the limit of the span, the limit of the material; and she is always balancing at the limit of the world, the limit of the ground—this idea of the periphery, the limit. So if we take into account these two elements, i.e., materiality and limit, we realize that they can be applied to everything that comprises our environment: it can be a landscape, it can be a glass house.

EA This is a lesson learned through engagement with archaeology: capturing transformations both material and atmospheric, through their transitions or limits.

JA It is very important since you have to deal with the invisible through the means of visibility. And we had a conversation about what is visible and what is not visible.

MM This is central in the discipline of architecture and especially in the world of structure: finding out what needs to be shown and what needs to be concealed. Coming back to the two points, the materiality and the limits, the photographer is looking at something that everybody sees, but nobody can see it the way that she does, through her eyes. So she is giving a meaning to something that might be unremarkable to the casual observer, something disconnected and singled out; then she places that into a context, recreating and interpreting the landscape in front of us. I'm very impressed by the idea that photography—like any other system, but we are talking about photography now—can be seen through its capacity to reveal the meaning of the things. And what I'm trying to do—through my work—is what Erieta is doing. So we are at this point where she is revealing through her means what I am trying to do with mine; she drapes a layer of thinking over the layer of building. And on top of everything else all this is done with an analog film camera; it is crazy this obsession with texture and materiality that extends even to the materiality of the final photograph on paper.

EA It is not only analog, but a 10 × 12 centimeter large-format camera with a panoramic back: this is because I am photographing in landscape orientation, since I see all architecture as landscape. The wide, horizontal format is not merely an aesthetic obsession for me. I see a square object and I photograph it in panoramic format because there is this underlying idea of the continuity of the landscape; the landscape brings everything together. While in a different context of work you could photograph via snapshots, I simply cannot do this; this kind of practice does not admit it. For example, it was September 2016 when I was introduced to the site, and Airtime was the first of Marc's buildings I photographed. At that point of course there was almost nothing, apart from a slab. Since that moment, because I was interested in Marc's work, the site was very intriguing for me to understand. That first day was cloudy and rainy: typical Parisian weather, just like with the whitish diffuse light that accompanies it. We could see the trains crossing and the new building slowly coming up, and I would try to visualize how the dialog would be built between the surrounding context and the yet unrealized architecture. Architects have their vision fleshed-out in detail, since they have internalized both the building and its construction sequence. But in my case, as an outsider, I had to build it from zero from the evolving site. Therefore, the more I would see it growing and connecting to the city in different ways, the more I wanted to understand and explain this specific location, which in a way is the generator of Marc's ideas.

JA Erieta, could you please tell us more about your distance, spatial distance, from your subjects? Because I am struck by the fact that most of your pictures are made from afar and almost never close-up.

EA I do not believe in close photographs except under very special circumstances. What interests me is the inversion of content and context, the flattening of hierarchies between objects and their environments, and in order to succeed in that you have to get distance from the object. Otherwise, if you move too close, you will miss this relationship with the context; you will amputate it. You might be able to reveal details, but never the connections, which is what interests me. This attitude of studying architecture through visual details has confused architecture photography because it promotes a fetishization of visual composition, with the result of emphasizing objects, shapes. Such an approach would never have worked with Marc's architecture, where it is important to allow the horizon and the light to unfold, the inside to blend with the outside.

MM You see, even the vocabulary she is using is the one I am using too. I told you I was almost more impressed by the landscape architect than by the architect. Because, what word were you using? Horizon? Also, the relationship with the Earth, the panoramic format. This is exactly what I am trying to do with my work. Last week I was in Germany to look at the landscape for a competition that we are doing there and I said to myself, "why should I go there?" I have Google, it should be enough. But then I reconsidered: I say to everybody, to my students, you have to be there at the site, and now I am not going to go myself? So I packed up and went, and I had a great experience. Because you feel the place, you feel the topography, and you feel the land and the earth. We are walking on the ground and we are erecting from the ground, so the idea of building is for me like a man who is lying down and then stands up; architecture is a relationship with gravity. It is a great relationship with gravity; you cannot avoid it.

JA You know there is an expression in French where we speak about the reality of the ground, as in "true ground." In your case you seem to have reached the true ground. It is important because if we try to understand the context, this is key.

MM All constructions exist in relation to the ground. Airtime is the only building to emphasize the difference between the real soil and the false soil; the way of resting on the ground is what melts the architecture into the context. It starts from the ground and it goes to the sky; there is no floating architecture, it does not exist. I really like this expression "true ground." So this idea that we are connected to the ground through $g = 9.81\,m/s^2$ is very important, and we cannot afford to forget that because our whole relationship to the ground is based on this. Erieta is revealing that in her way and I'm trying to look at my way through her photographs. It is the first time I am attempting such introspection with a photographer, and maybe the last one.

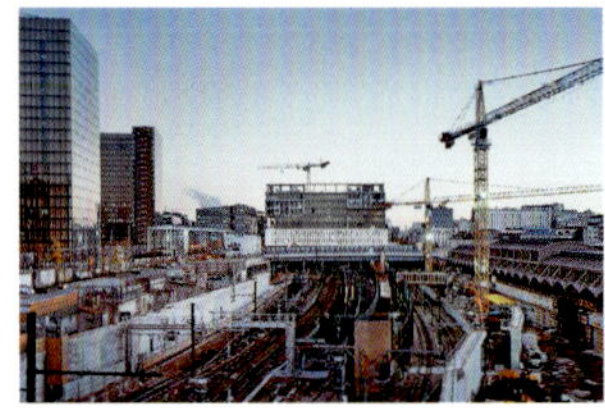
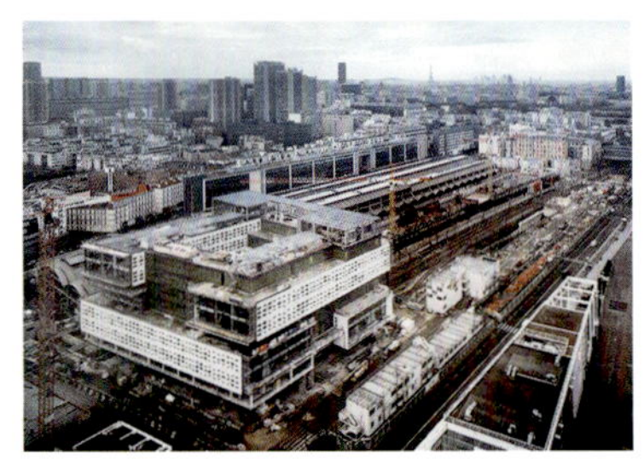
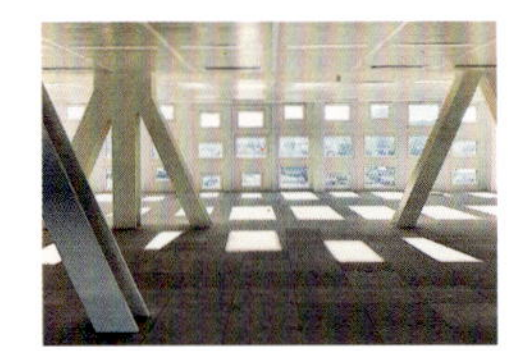
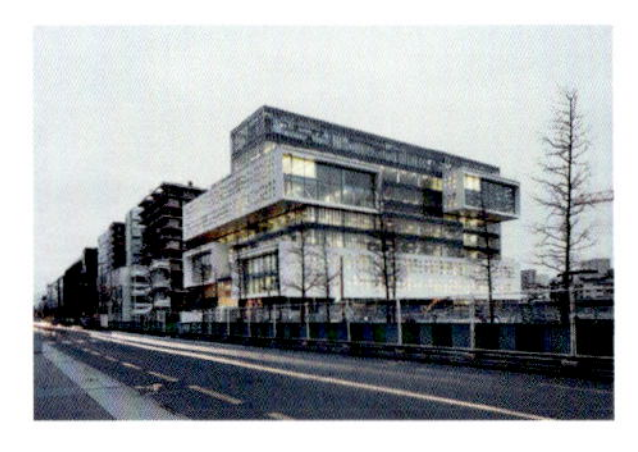
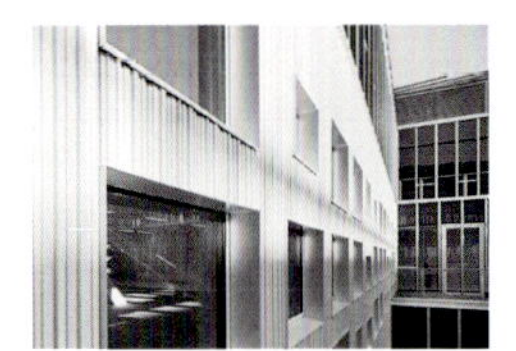
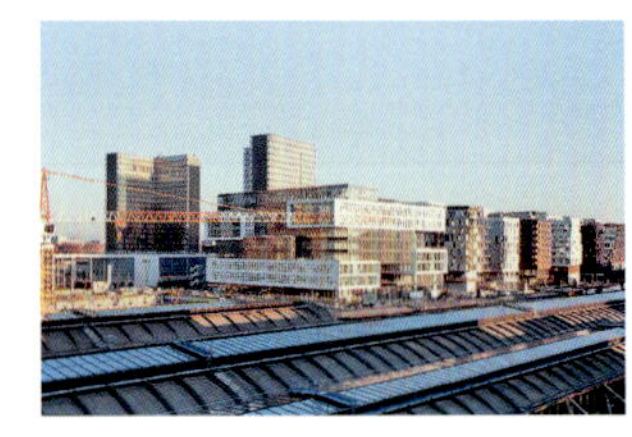
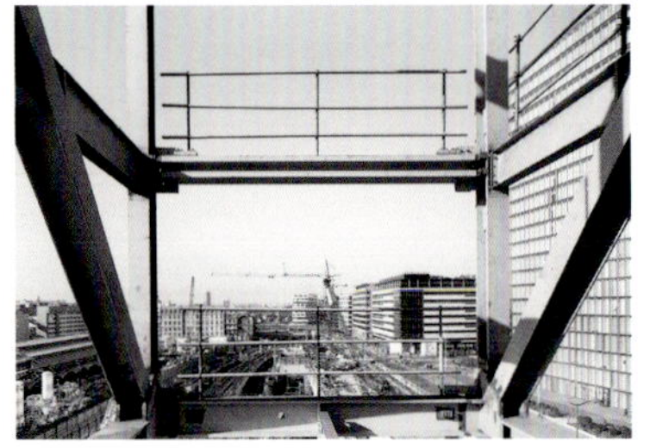
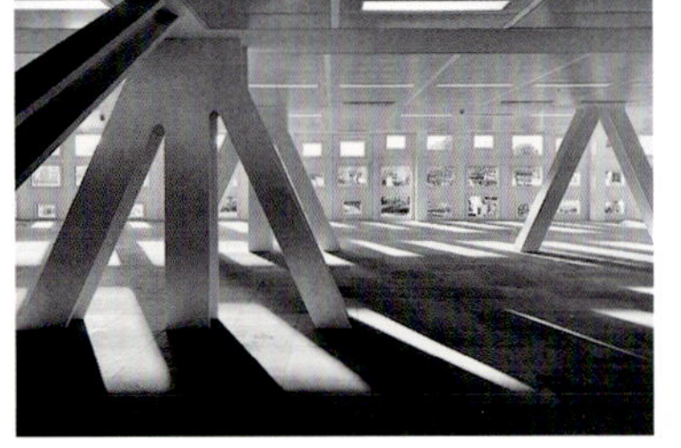
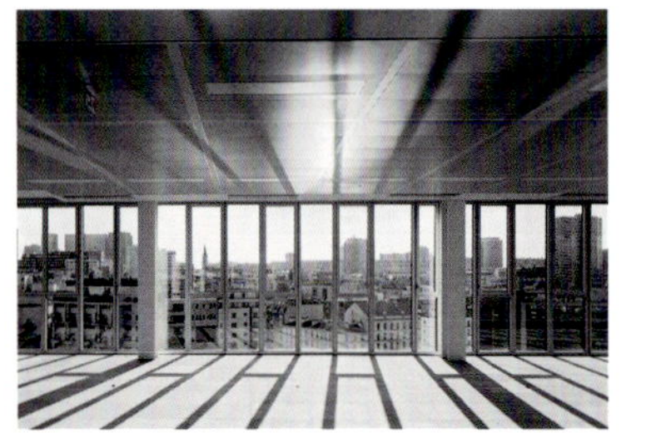
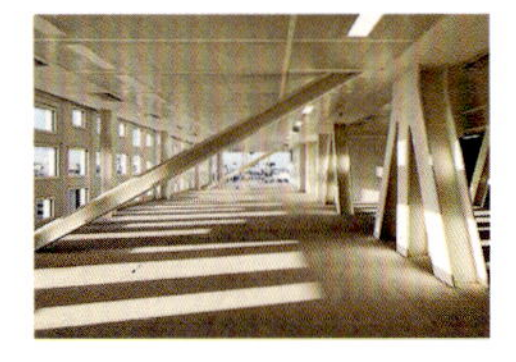
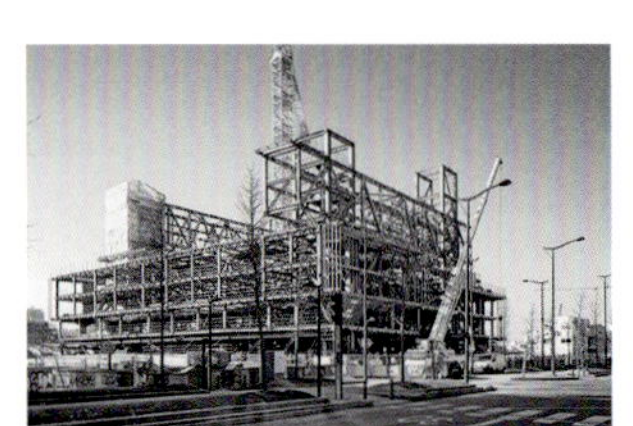
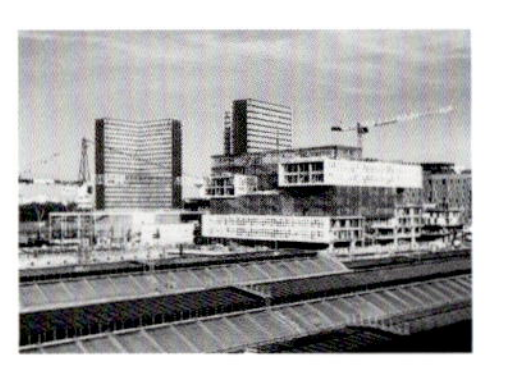
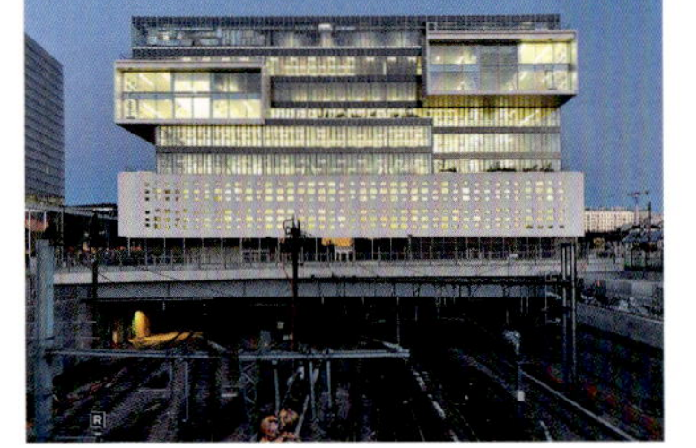
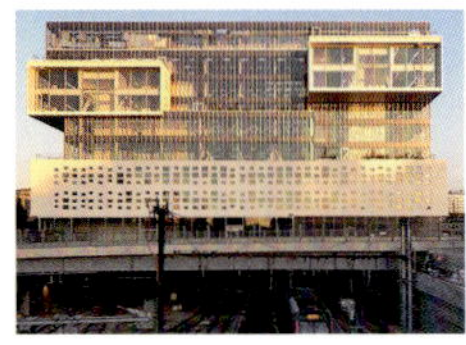
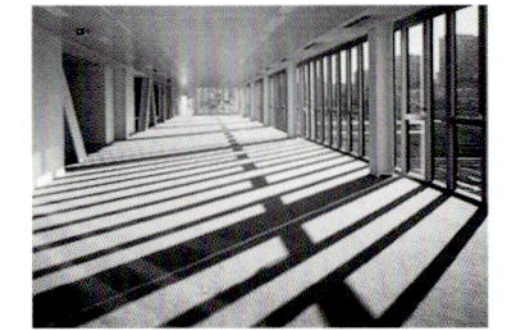

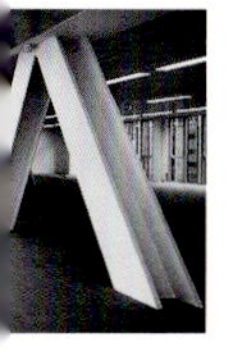
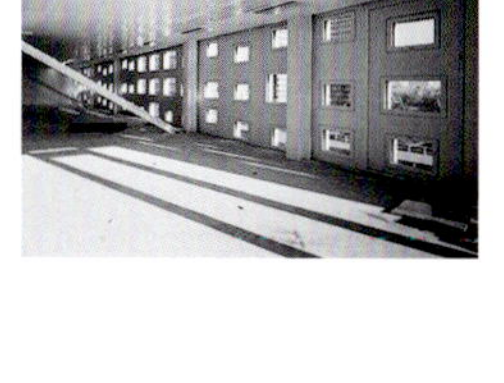
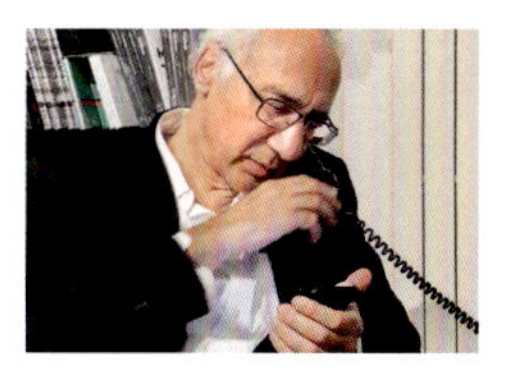
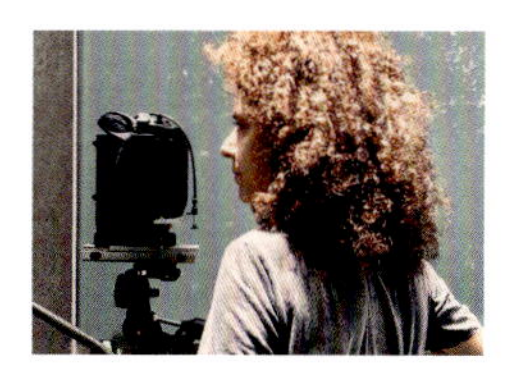
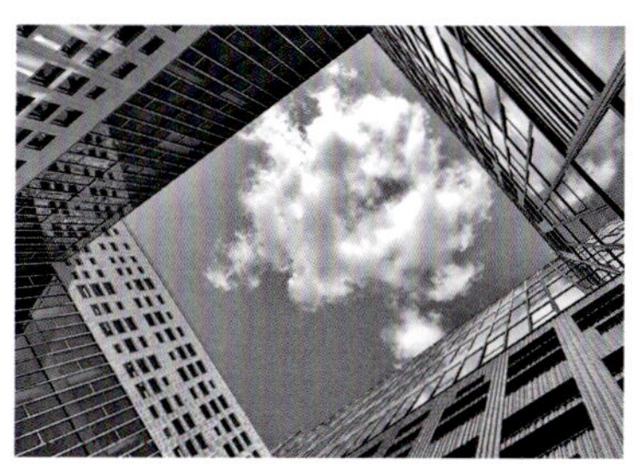
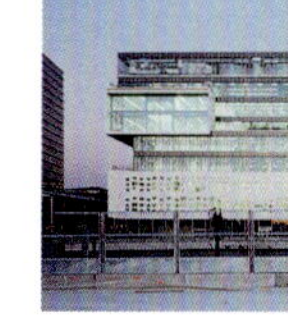
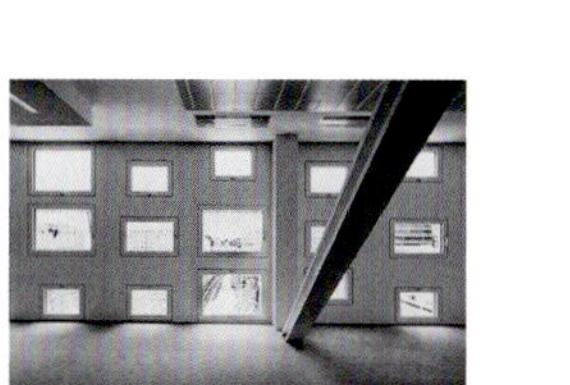
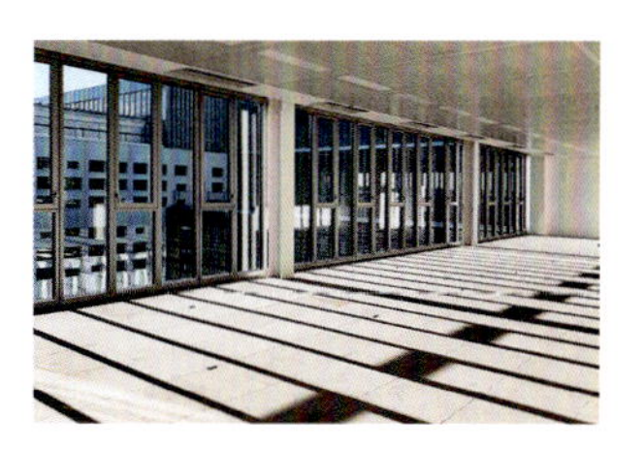
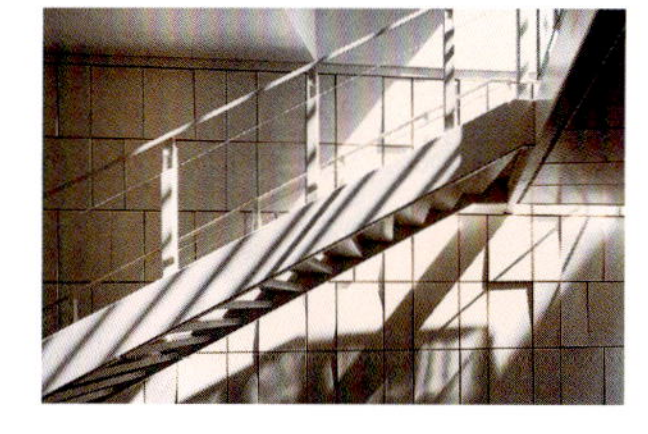
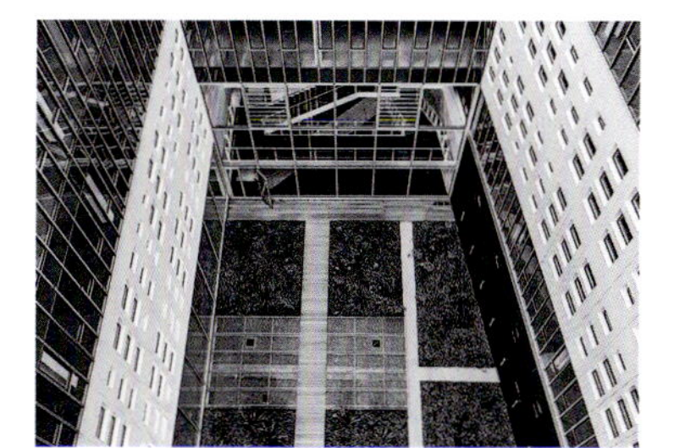
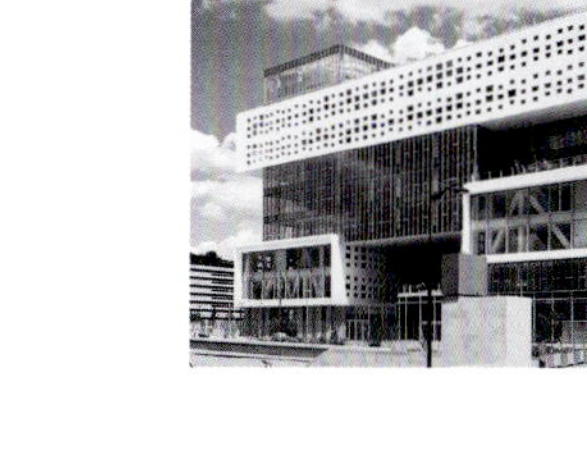
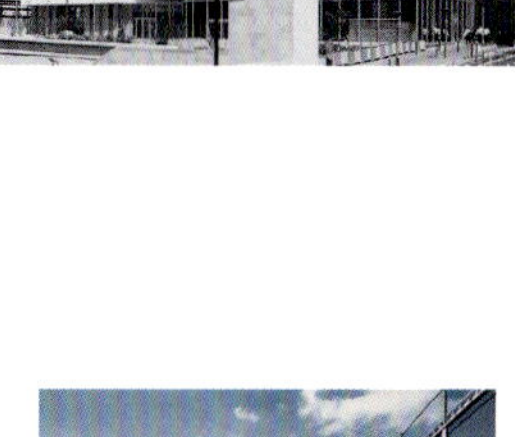
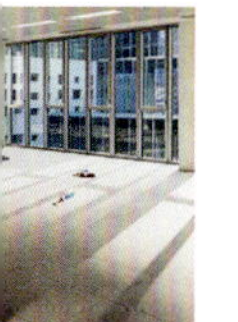
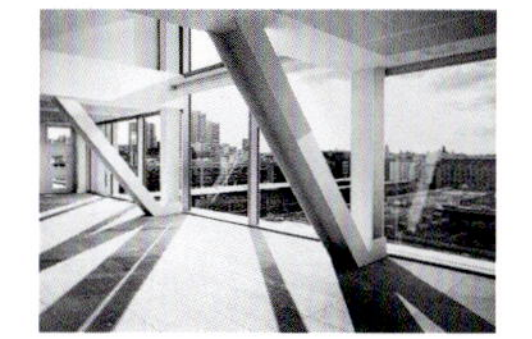
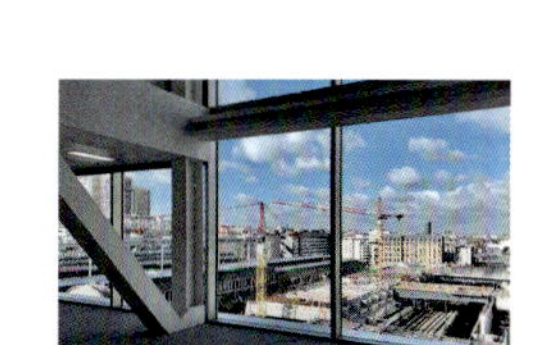
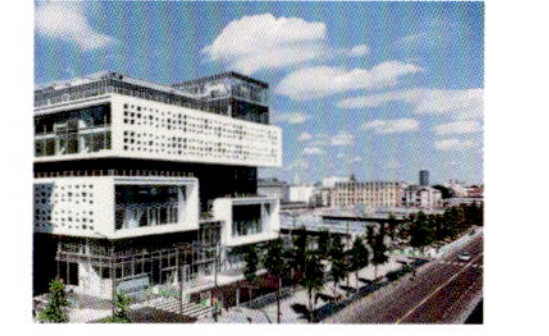
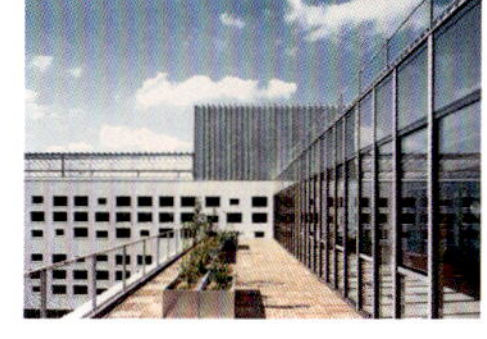

Biography Marc Mimram
Architect, Engineer

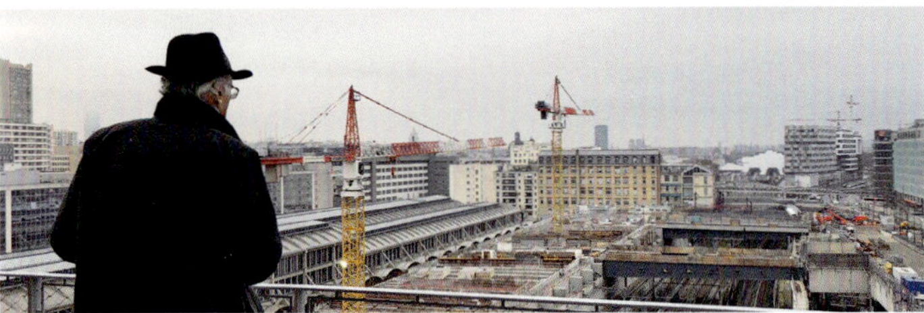

Marc Mimram (b. 1955, Paris) has a master's degree in mathematics from the Université Paris VII (1976), an engineering diploma from the École Nationale des Ponts et Chaussées (1978), a master's degree in civil engineering from the University of California, Berkeley (1979), an architecture diploma (DPLG) from the École Nationale Supérieure des Beaux Arts in Paris (1980), and a postgraduate degree in philosophy from the Université Paris I Panthéon-Sorbonne (1982). He founded his own consultancy and architecture and engineering firm in 1992.

He has been an architect-engineer since 1981, and has completed many civil engineering structures and architectural projects in France and abroad, including bridges in France (Solférino Footbridge, Paris), in Germany (Strasbourg—Kehl), in Morocco (Rabat—Salé), which won the Aga Khan Award, in China (Beijing, Tianjin, Yangzhou), large sport facilities (Roland-Garros Stadium, Paris), and infrastructure buildings (Airtime, Paris, and Montpellier Railway Station, France).

Mimram has taught at the École des Ponts et Chaussées in Paris, the École Polytechnique Fédérale in Lausanne, and Princeton University in the United States. He was appointed a Professor of Architectural Schools and currently teaches at the École d'Architecture de Marne-la-Vallée near Paris.

He has published several books, such as *Structure et Formes* (Paris, 1983); *Passerelle Solférino* (Basel, 2001); *Architettura Ibrida* (Milan, 2009); and *Marc Mimram: Architecture & Structure* (Munich, 2015). He has given numerous lectures all over the world, including lectures at Harvard University, Cornell University, Princeton, Tokyo University, as well as São Paulo, Venice, and Oslo.

In his work as an architect and an engineer, Marc Mimram has shown an interest in architecture that is intelligently built through the development of considered structures that relate to landscape, light, and materials. He feels that his work is about an attentive and generous transformation of the matter of which the world is made. In his hands architecture becomes an art of transformation, and materiality becomes the expression of culture.

Image: © Erieta Attali

Biography Erieta Attali
Landscape and Architecture Photographer

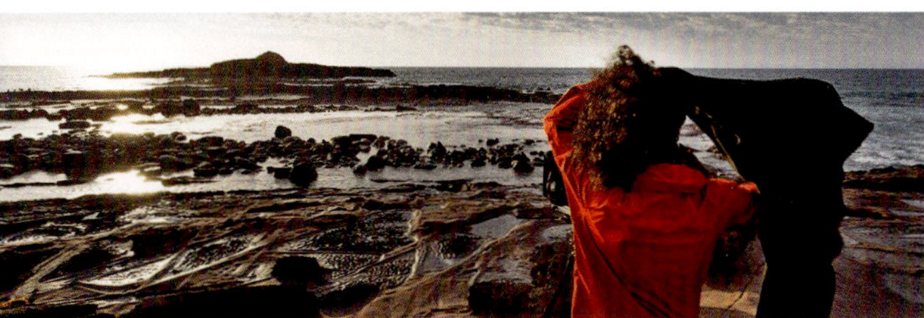

Erieta Attali was born in Tel Aviv and grew up in Istanbul and Athens. She currently resides between New York and Paris, photographing the work of contemporary architects from around the world. Attali began her photographic career in 1993 as a landscape and archaeology photographer with a specialty in underground burial sites. During the past twenty years she has been preoccupied primarily with architectural and landscape photography, with a body of work spanning from Europe to the Americas and from Asia to Australia, sponsored by national and academic institutions globally. Her work has been shown in several exhibitions and is the subject of many monographs. The National Gallery of Victoria (NGV) in Melbourne, Australia, has acquired her work for its permanent collection. After receiving her master's in photography from Goldsmiths, University of London, Attali continued her studies as visiting scholar at the Graduate School of Architecture, Planning and Preservation, Columbia University, in New York, with support of the Fulbright Foundation, and at Waseda University, Tokyo, with the support of the Japan Foundation. She holds a PhD from the School of Architecture and Design, RMIT University, Melbourne, Australia. Attali has taught architectural photography at GSAPP, Columbia University as an adjunct assistant professor between 2003 and 2018. She has been a visiting professor at the Technical University of Munich (TUM) Faculty of Architecture, The Catholic University of Chile, School of Architecture, the Royal Danish Academy of Arts in Copenhagen, Architectural Association in London, RMIT in Melbourne, University of Tokyo, Technion in Haifa, Israel, and the University of Sydney among others. Attali is currently a research fellow at the Académie d'architecture in Paris and an artist-in-residence at the Cité internationale des arts conducting a photographic survey on Paris and the Seine. She is the author and editor of numerous books such as *Glass | Wood: Erieta Attali on Kengo Kuma* and *Periphery | Archaeology of Light*, published by Hatje Cantz, Berlin, among others.

Image: © Rondo Wei

Biography Jean Attali

Jean Attali is emeritus professor at École Nationale Supérieure d'Architecture Paris-Malaquais. As a philosopher, for years he has been dedicating his work, teaching, and research to architecture and urbanism. From 2007 to 2016 he led a research seminar, and has created a collective atlas on the worldwide urban landscape, edited online and to be published soon in a book format. He has also published extensively on a large array of topics, from architecture and urbanism to contemporary art and photography, as well as urban geography: *Le plan et le détail: Une philosophie de l'architecture et de la ville* (Nîmes, 2001), *Retours de mer* (Paris, 2014), and *Elements Europa: European Council and Council of the European Union* (Brussels, 2016), with Philippe Samyn, are among his books.

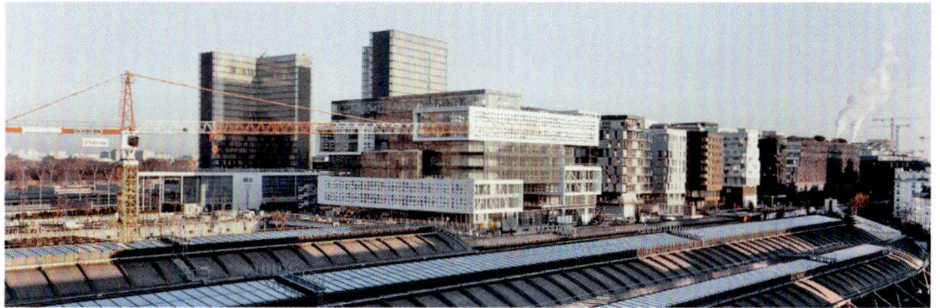

Bâtiment Airtime | → p.10

Marc Mimram

Entre l'avenue de France et la halle Freyssinet coule le fleuve ferroviaire, avec ses variations de largeurs et de contraintes.

Ici, au droit du bâtiment Airtime, la portée possible sans appuis intermédiaires est de 58 mètres. Partout ailleurs, les bâtiments qui se développent au-dessus du réseau ferroviaire ont été implantés sur une dalle épaisse, une table de béton sur laquelle peut s'installer de manière aléatoire et non définie préalablement n'importe quel assemblage de bâtiments contenus dans les règles d'urbanisme. Les urbanistes ont abandonné la *tabula rasa* pour la *tabula nova*; une dalle en attente d'urbanisation. Ce dispositif est irrationnel et peu économe. En outre, il ne peut pas être transposé au droit du projet car la portée y est trop importante et les appuis intermédiaires impossibles à moins d'une restructuration fort onéreuse du plateau ferroviaire.

Notre proposition inverse le processus : au lieu d'une installation sur une dalle en attente, nous avons proposé de suspendre la dalle de couverture des voies ferrées au bâtiment-pont. Cette hypothèse nouvelle modifie l'équation économique et permet d'intégrer le coût de la structure invisible de la dalle dans la superstructure du bâtiment et, par là même, de requalifier son architecture au regard de cette disposition géographique particulière.

Le bâtiment ainsi projeté devient un bâtiment-pont appuyé de part et d'autre du plateau ferroviaire à 58 mètres de distance, ses 16 000 tonnes étant suspendues au-dessus des trains. Ce dispositif structurel s'avère néanmoins libérateur et permet de transformer la contrainte gravitaire en une situation d'usage particulière. Puisque les contraintes sont concentrées dans les étages intégrant la structure de franchissement, les autres parties du bâtiment sont libres. Suspendues à la structure principale ou supportées par elle, elles peuvent varier d'épaisseur et dégager des terrasses, des balcons, des loggias, des mezzanines – autant de prolongements de l'espace de travail qui qualifient celui-ci selon les orientations et les vues.

Le dispositif structurel adopté permet de développer une domesticité de l'espace tertiaire : les lieux et les espaces prolongeant ceux du bureau s'ouvrent sur la ville ou en sont protégés par les encorbellements de la structure pour qualifier les lieux de travail en leur offrant des extensions partagées et appropriables. Paradoxalement, ce dispositif très généreux est issu de la contrainte structurelle du franchissement et de la résolution de l'équation ferroviaire consistant à intégrer la dalle de couverture plutôt que de la faire peser sur l'économie du projet sous la forme d'une dalle de support inefficace.

L'architecture devient alors plus cohérente, et la situation structurelle est évoquée sans ostension. Demain, la présence du plateau ferroviaire s'effacera sous la couverture de l'ensemble du réseau, mais le dispositif adopté continuera d'évoquer cette situation extraordinaire. Les poutres du grand franchissement sont concentrées dans les étages aux façades percées selon une densité évoquant la poutre Vierendeel utilisée. Les étages portés et suspendus sont libres dans la variation des terrasses qu'ils accueillent. La mémoire du processus de fabrication comme celle du chantier s'incarnent dans une architecture qui ne montre pas nécessairement ses muscles, mais se présente sans camouflage, sans renier une condition initiale géographique déterminante. C'est bien cette mise en cohérence qui fait projet, et son expression construite fait architecture.

S'approprier l'horizon urbain

Le projet tertiaire développé entre la Bibliothèque de France et la halle Freyssinet franchit les voies de chemin de fer. Pour autant, il ne doit pas s'affranchir du paysage urbain auquel il appartient, bien au contraire. Nous voulons que la situation de franchissement ancre le projet dans le territoire du XIIIe arrondissement, dans cette magnifique topographie géographique et construite, depuis l'horizon des tours de la porte d'Italie jusqu'à la butte aux Cailles, entre les Gobelins et la Salpêtrière et, plus loin, vers Ivry et Gentilly. C'est ce territoire qui s'offre de manière tout à fait exceptionnelle depuis le bâtiment. C'est ce dialogue qui doit s'ouvrir avec le bâtiment et fonder son architecture : offrons ce panorama en partage.

Dans le développement du quartier Paris Rive Gauche, et particulièrement le long de l'avenue de France, le projet occupe une place très spécifique. Au nord-est, il s'ouvre sur les tours de la Bibliothèque de France, vers le parc de Bercy, dans l'axe de la passerelle qui franchit la Seine. Ce lien est d'autant plus fort qu'il marque la déclivité du sol ici et ancre la nouvelle rive gauche au-dessus des voies du XIIIe historique.
Le projet propose de créer à partir des contraintes du franchissement de nouvelles conditions d'usage pour un bâtiment tertiaire, en dialogue avec la ville.
Telle est la situation qui a guidé notre recherche structurelle et morphologique. Le projet tire profit d'une structure d'exception qui renvoie davantage à l'ouvrage d'art qu'au bâtiment, pour générer à son tour des situations d'exception. La structure nécessaire au franchissement donne une grande liberté de forme à l'enveloppe et permet, selon les opportunités spécifiques du site et les vues qu'elle offre, de disposer de lieux d'usage adressés au paysage urbain environnant: balcons filants, *open spaces* double hauteur, terrasses, cadrages.

L'environnement comme condition d'usage

Nous voulons que le dialogue avec la ville soit au centre du développement du projet. À cette situation qui permet de voir s'ajoute par un effet de miroir la possibilité d'être vu. Le bâtiment qui prend place ici ne s'inscrit pas seulement dans un alignement, mais aussi dans des perspectives remarquables. La ville, l'horizon, le ciel, mais aussi les lumières, les orientations sont des conditions environnementales, et nous voulons que celles-ci guident les nouveaux usages tertiaires que propose le projet.
La situation spécifique d'immeuble-pont permet de désolidariser les éléments de franchissement – les grandes poutres-ponts de 58 mètres de portée – des éléments portés comme des éléments suspendus.
Ainsi, grâce à la distinction avec ces grandes structures, ce sont des terrasses, des doubles hauteurs, des loggias qui viennent se glisser entre les éléments structuraux.
L'occupation tertiaire sort alors de sa logique géométrique (trame de 1,35 mètre et épaisseur de 18 mètres, avec noyau central non éclairé} pour découvrir des dimensions nouvelles, variables de 6 à 19 mètres d'épaisseur, des bureaux traversants, des plateaux libres aux façades différentes, des prolongements extérieurs.
Nous proposons ici de reconsidérer les conditions et de profiter de la liberté offerte par les grands franchissements pour créer de nouvelles conditions de travail dans le tertiaire. L'univers des bureaux est un produit trop normé. L'occasion nous est donnée d'innover et de proposer de nouveaux modes de travail variables, adaptés, différenciés. Il s'agit de sortir de l'unique trame banalisée pour créer de véritables lieux de travail ouverts sur la ville, qui puissent être prolongés par des lieux partagés – lieux de rencontre horizontaux comme les terrasses abritées ou balcons verticaux comme les mezzanines. Créer de la convivialité au travail, offrir des dispositifs qui permettront d'être ensemble dans de meilleures conditions de vie: le projet le permet et ouvre la voie à de nouvelles pratiques dans le monde tertiaire.
Le bâtiment transforme les contraintes de franchissement en variations sur les usages. La qualité environnementale est ici celle des utilisations, des orientations et des ouvertures sur l'horizon de la ville. Le projet se creuse, se façonne à mesure des possibilités offertes par la structure pour l'orienter dans le paysage urbain.

Un équilibre stabilisé

La contrainte de franchissement de grande portée au-dessus de l'espace ferroviaire pourrait inciter à transformer le bâtiment en édifice compact, massif, ancré sur ses appuis préfondés. Nous avons souhaité *a contrario* évoquer le chemin gravitaire dans ses capacités d'assemblages sophistiqués, avec des membrures soulevées du sol évoquant un «équilibre stabilisé».
Les éléments porteurs sont de deux natures, les éléments des franchissements de grande portée se distinguant de ceux des liens constituant les portiques transversaux. Si les éléments porteurs sont tous liés et indissociables, ils apparaissent pourtant désolidarisés les uns des autres. Leur assemblage se fait au cœur de l'édifice sur les noyaux d'escaliers qui servent de transfert des charges verticales.
Ici, nous avons souhaité mettre en suspension le bâtiment. La structure de franchissement n'est pas issue d'une simple contrainte de portée, c'est un élément libérateur qui fixe les directions des grandes poutres principales décollées pour offrir des vues et des assemblages multiples. Les grandes poutres d'apparence disjointe sont assemblées pour constituer des portiques, des ensembles composés et stabilisés autour des noyaux centraux, puis les charges sont renvoyées sur les deux lignes d'appui situées sur l'avenue de France et le long de la promenade plantée au sud.
Nous n'avons pas voulu d'expressionnisme structural exacerbé mais une force donnée aux éléments de franchissement par l'ordonnancement des composants du projet.
La structure est ici au service du dialogue entre urbanité et usage. C'est elle qui libère le panorama. C'est elle qui fait varier les usages.
La massivité en suspens de ces grands éléments structuraux permet d'interroger à nouveau l'expression des chemins gravitaires de manière plus sensible aux plaisirs du lieu, plus généreuse face aux plaisirs d'être là.
Le travail sur les façades renvoie à la dualité entre ce qui porte et ce qui est porté. Les ponts, les éléments de franchissement traduisent les contraintes auxquelles ils sont soumis par une enveloppe unitaire et massive dont la perforation varie au rythme de la courbe des efforts qui transitent dans la poutre de façade. Les parties posées ou suspendues qui se glissent entre les volumes porteurs sont l'expression d'une absence de contraintes, d'une grande légèreté qui se manifeste à travers une peau de verre, un mur rideau simple, unitaire. Le contraste entre ces deux natures d'enveloppe place les éléments porteurs dans une situation de suspension.

Les conditions d'appui forment ici une contrainte majeure du projet. Elles sont prédéfinies géométriquement, statiquement et dimensionnellement. Pour ne pas en faire l'expression centrale d'un projet qui doit bien plutôt s'adresser à la ville et s'adapter à l'échelle du passant, les appuis sont inscrits dans un dispositif qui, à grande échelle, évoque l'équilibre stabilisé et, localement, intègre le transfert de charge à une géométrie simple. La prouesse est visible, mais elle n'est pas omniprésente. Les ordres de lecture du bâtiment l'inscrivent dans les échelles de la ville.

Un chantier partagé

Le chantier est achevé. Les nuits de lancement des structures de franchissement au-dessus des voies se sont écoulées lentement au rythme d'un ouvrage d'art. Le *crash deck* formé par la dalle portée au-dessus des voies ferrées est désormais suspendu aux poutres principales. Les grandes structures de franchissement concentrent dans les appuis espacés de 58 mètres (deux sur l'avenue de France, quatre sur la promenade plantée) les charges gravitaires déconcentrées sur 199 boîtes à ressorts qui s'interposent pour supprimer les vibrations ferroviaires. Les 16 000 tonnes de l'édifice se diffusent doucement.
La structure vit, se déforme, reprend sa contre-flèche et se déforme au fur et à mesure de ses occupations variables. Quelques centimètres vers le haut, jusqu'à 12 centimètres vers le bas. Cela paraît peu : la structure est rigide. Et cela paraît beaucoup, les accès se faisant directement depuis les rues.
Rigidité et souplesse – les façades sont elles-mêmes suspendues pour permettre cette déformation aléatoire et maîtrisée.
Le bâtiment ne vibre pas et semble indifférent aux passages des trains.
Les bureaux s'ouvrent sur de longues terrasses qui prolongent les espaces de travail dans toutes les directions du regard urbain, proche et lointain : bancs, plantations et prises électriques devraient rendre plus domestiques, plus empathiques, des bureaux trop souvent cloisonnés.

Sous les encorbellements, sur le fleuve, entre les tours de la Bibliothèque, au loin vers Notre-Dame et la tour Eiffel, plus près sur les tours du XIIIe – partout le regard accompagne des pratiques nouvelles qu'une trame construite normative semblait pour toujours standardiser.
Ce bâtiment n'est pas standard, la vie au travail ne devrait pas l'être. À tel point que l'on cherche le bureau de la direction : pas d'axialité, pas de figure tutélaire, pas de direction pour la direction. Pas d'étage type mais une proposition d'ouverture, une complexité informée par les orientations, les vues, les profondeurs, les occupations variables au gré des modes d'habiter au travail.
Dans les transparences de la cour intérieure, les espaces suspendus dialoguent en légèreté au-dessus de la cour plantée sous laquelle les trains ont disparu.

Une construction en mémoire

> Mémoire du passage des trains,
> Mémoire des hommes évoluant dans l'ossature arachnéenne,
> Mémoire du travail concentré dans cette matière informée en construction, transformée en protection, ordonnée en architecture.

L'architecture est issue de la matière du monde ainsi métamorphosée en matière à penser les espaces à vivre. La structure est réglée par la résistance des matériaux.
Les images mentales sont en mémoire, celle des plaisirs de la fabrication dans la dureté du chantier. L'architecture est cette projection mentale, celle de nos dessins métamorphosée en nature ordonnée, en structure équilibrée, en espace bâti. Les images du projet en témoignent, nous avons voulu les partager dans le grain des textures argentiques, dans les évolutions du caché au visible, du brut au fini.
Une mémoire construite en partage. Une histoire unique.

Une conversation | → p. 74
Marc Mimram, Erieta Attali et Jean Attali

JA La plupart des gens se retrouvent piégés dans le monde des images. Ce que je veux dire par « piégés », c'est qu'ils se sont habitués à regarder l'image en surface plutôt qu'en profondeur, même si le pouvoir de la photographie réside dans le fait qu'elle dirige l'attention des gens vers le cœur du sujet. Donc, quand nous parlons d'images, et de photographies d'architecture en particulier, il faut insister sur le fait que le but ne devrait pas être de regarder l'image en tant que telle mais plutôt de regarder quelque chose à travers l'image, à travers la vision d'un autre.

MM Oui, il y a toujours ce danger qu'on regarde l'image elle-même au lieu d'essayer de comprendre l'œuvre par le biais de l'image. Mais je veux bien prendre ce risque car j'espère qu'on ira au-delà de la surface de l'image, qu'on ira plus loin.

JA La façon dont on doit approcher cette série photographique est pour moi sans équivoque. Je veux dire par là que la relation entre deux images n'est pas la relation entre deux cadrages, par exemple la ligne d'horizon ou une colline. Il est très important d'attirer l'attention du spectateur sur la vision et non sur l'image en tant qu'artefact. Et cela commence par ce que vous voyez : ce n'est pas le bâtiment en tant que tel que l'on voit mais la relation de ce bâtiment à son environnement.

EA L'objet de la photographie n'est pas ce que l'on regarde, mais l'acte même de regarder à travers ce qui est photographié. Et c'est ce qui fait que la photographie d'architecture est à la fois intentionnelle et conséquentielle dans son appréhension de l'espace bâti. Certains photographes sont attirés par les formes, par ce que l'on pourrait appeler un maniérisme de l'image : ils en viennent à photographier l'architecture d'une façon qui peut produire des compositions intéressantes mais, en fin de compte, ils font des contresens, ils nous induisent en erreur. Le simple fait que cela puisse arriver nous montre à quel point il est important de ne pas regarder l'image, mais de regarder à travers elle.

JA Absolument. Je pense que l'image et l'architecture sont toutes deux plus intéressantes si elles servent de focales. Et dans le projet Airtime, il est évident que la position des différentes terrasses et niveaux permet cette vision traversante, cette vision qui va de l'intérieur vers l'extérieur, de la structure du bâtiment vers l'environnement urbain.

EA Ce bâtiment est un dispositif permettant de se connecter aux différentes vues et en même temps un espace dans lequel évoluer, si bien que la distinction entre intérieur et extérieur disparaît. Quelque part, j'ai aussi l'impression qu'on y est à la fois enraciné et déraciné ; cela crée une atmosphère multidimensionnelle. Bien sûr, quand toutes les voies de chemin de fer seront recouvertes, on ne se souviendra peut-être plus des gens qui travaillaient ici ni de la profondeur de cet espace ouvert, mais au moins, ce processus en constante évolution de mise en relation du bâtiment avec la ville sera préservé grâce aux photographies.

MM Il y a non seulement, comme Erieta aime à le souligner, une relation entre le bâtiment et le paysage, mais toute l'idée qui sous-tend cette structure est aussi celle d'un dispositif qui devrait offrir la possibilité et la liberté de voir. Comprendre cela a été un moment déterminant pour moi. Vous vous souvenez peut-être de notre première conversation à ce sujet : quand vous êtes à l'intérieur des deux barres blanches, la structure encadre votre appréhension de la ville ; et quand vous êtes à l'extérieur de la structure, vous êtes totalement libres. La première chose que nous avons faite pour le concours a été d'utiliser un ballon pour prendre des photos depuis différents points de vue afin de voir ce que les gens verraient.

EA Dans les dernières séries de photos que nous avons regardées avec Marc, il y en a quelques-unes où espaces intérieur et extérieur se confondent en une sorte de paysage nuageux. Vous flottez et vous percevez le contexte urbain dissous à travers cet environnement structurel. Nous avons aussi eu la chance de pouvoir photographier l'endroit avant l'arrivée du mobilier : l'intérieur était alors une extension du paysage où tout se déroulait à une échelle urbaine. Ce continuum aurait été interrompu si le mobilier avait été présent au premier plan.

MM Cette idée de flottaison est très intéressante. Je me suis aussi demandé comment les gens allaient ressentir le fait qu'ils étaient dans un bâtiment d'une portée de 58 mètres ? Est-ce qu'ils allaient avoir l'impression d'être connectés au terrain ? Il y a six points de connexion au terrain : quatre sur un côté et deux sur l'autre. Est-ce que cela va créer une différence ? Je pense que oui. Je pense que nous avons instinctivement un sens de l'espace qui nous entoure, quel que soit l'endroit où nous sommes.

JA Je me souviens de ce que j'ai ressenti dans les appartements de l'Unité d'habitation de Le Corbusier, où le bâtiment a une portée de seize mètres, plus les deux balcons, ce qui fait dix-huit mètres en tout. Le ressenti de cette distance revêt une grande importance. Donc les 58 mètres dont tu parles, c'est une façon d'amplifier considérablement ce ressenti.

MM Le ressenti de l'espace mais aussi de la pesanteur. Et il y a un autre élément : la dimension domestique des espaces de travail, grâce aux volumes en double hauteur et aux terrasses. L'architecture nous offre ici une expérience très différente : dans des circonstances habituelles, ce genre d'immeuble de bureaux aurait une largeur de dix-huit mètres avec deux longs couloirs courant parallèlement à la façade. Or ici, nous avons une largeur qui va de neuf à dix-huit mètres, ce qui signifie que nous avons la possibilité de mettre des terrasses où nous voulons.

JA Marc, est-ce que tu peux revenir sur ce que tu appelles la dimension domestique ? Ton bâtiment présente en effet le paradoxe d'introduire cet aspect dans un environnement de bureaux. Je pense que c'est très important parce que l'expérience de l'espace commence pour tout le monde par l'expérience du chez-soi. L'expérience spatiale prend ses racines dans le fait de se sentir chez soi, avec ou sans confort. C'est là la relation originelle entre notre corps et l'espace, et pour moi, c'est là que commence l'architecture. Quand tu parles de la dimension domestique de cet immeuble de bureaux, c'est donc le point le plus essentiel pour moi.

MM Vous connaissez la thèse de Marc-Antoine Laugier sur le fait que l'architecture est liée à la cabane rustique... Il y a beaucoup de gens qui soutiennent que c'est là le point de départ de l'architecture. Mais qu'en est-il de la cabane d'aujourd'hui ? Nous passons douze heures par jour chez nous, dont sept à dormir, ce qui fait cinq heures réelles à la maison, alors que nous en passons huit au bureau. Alors où est notre maison ? Vous savez ce qu'est la dimension domestique dans un bureau ? Ce sont des gens qui colonisent l'espace avec leurs biens personnels, leurs vies qui se déroulent dans un chaos animé : c'est le son d'un piano, des livres dispersés partout, etc. C'est ici que se loge la dimension domestique. Dans ce bâtiment, Airtime, la relation entre intérieur et extérieur sera complètement différente de celle qui caractérise un immeuble de bureaux classique. Dans les autres immeubles de bureaux, vous êtes toujours à l'intérieur ; à New York vous ne pouvez même pas ouvrir une fenêtre. Mais ici, non seulement vous pouvez ouvrir une fenêtre, mais cette fenêtre rejoint la terrasse, et la terrasse est immense. J'espère que les gens seront connectés à la terrasse, connectés à la vue et connectés au monde. S'ils ont à travailler dans ce monde, pour moi ils doivent être connectés à ce monde. Ils ne peuvent pas être à la bourse, comme à Wall Street, dans la pénombre, uniquement concentrés sur l'achat, la vente et la négociation. Nous devons être connectés au monde. C'est là le principal pouvoir transformateur de l'architecture.

JA Évidemment, mais cette relation au monde, cet élan vers le monde, commence ou puise ses racines dans cette expérience primitive du chez-soi, dans cette idée qu'on se situe quelque part dans le monde.

L'importance d'être relié aux autres dans les limites d'un espace spécifique est à la base même de l'expérience architecturale. Et si l'on veut que les gens soient plus sensibles à l'architecture, il est primordial de transmettre cette idée d'expérience personnelle aux ouvriers. C'est pourquoi cette dimension domestique du bâtiment dont tu parlais me passionne. Je voudrais demander à Erieta ce qu'elle pense de cet aspect domestique. Je sais que c'est un sujet très paradoxal. Erieta, j'aimerais aussi savoir quelle est ton expérience dans la pratique.

EA Dans ma vie quotidienne, je ne crois pas être attachée à une routine spécifique liée à un espace en particulier. Je dirais plutôt que chaque espace devient ma maison. Je ne me sens jamais étrangère quand j'arrive dans un lieu : c'est un processus que j'ai développé au fil du temps, après être passée plusieurs fois d'une maison, d'un type de travail, d'un espace à l'autre.

MM Et c'est la même chose avec les paysages ?

EA Absolument. En particulier depuis que j'ai commencé à photographier : le processus photographique me permet de développer un lien très fort avec les lieux dans lesquels je me retrouve pour la première fois.

MM Tu photographies aussi des maisons, des bâtiments.

EA Oui, mais j'éprouve toujours une certaine difficulté à entrer dans des intérieurs remplis d'objets personnels. Cela crée chez moi à la fois de la gêne et de la distraction. C'est pourquoi je préfère les espaces collectifs. Mes photographies de projets publics ou institutionnels véhiculent mieux mon langage visuel. La première chose à faire, c'est d'étudier le contexte, puis de comprendre le bâtiment lui-même, mais tout commence par le contexte. Je me promène dans les rues alentour, je rentre et je ressors, je passe du temps avec le bâtiment. C'est ce que nous avons fait au Maroc pour le pont, Marc s'en souvient. Un jour il m'a dit : « Aujourd'hui on a marché douze kilomètres pour faire cinq photos, ensuite on a fait des kilomètres et des kilomètres, et finalement on n'a même pas utilisé ces photos. » Mais c'est ce que je fais quand je veux comprendre un site. J'ai aussi une approche collective des photographies : il ne s'agit pas tant de clichés individuels que d'un puzzle que je dois assembler, d'une mosaïque. Quand je pense à toutes ces images que j'ai faites, je les visualise toutes ensemble. Elles ne sont jamais isolées, elles sont rassemblées en plusieurs groupes. Et bien souvent, dans ces séries d'images, les espaces vides entre les images elles-mêmes sont tout aussi importants. Ils permettent de bâtir un rythme de lecture et de compréhension.

JA Cette notion d'espace vacant ou d'intervalle me fait penser à l'importance du vide, à la fois au sens spatial et esthétique, mais aussi dans ton approche de la réalité. Et cela a pour moi quelque chose de très judaïque : Dieu n'est pas là, donc cela veut dire que, dans un monde qui n'est pas entier, nous avons cet intérêt pour le vide. Il y a cette présence du vide : une présence de l'absence. Je pense que cela nourrit et alimente la démarche architecturale de Marc. Est-ce que tu vois les choses comme ça ?

MM Je dois dire que je suis assez stupéfait car le vide est en fait la chose la plus importante dans le domaine de l'ingénierie. Robert le Ricolais disait : « Ne mettez pas de la matière mais des vides dans la structure. » L'idée d'inertie, qui est la plus déterminante en matière de résistance d'une structure, correspond à l'idée de vide. Du point de vue de l'ingénierie, l'espace le plus important dans lequel je sois jamais entré est le dôme de Brunelleschi dans la cathédrale de Florence, *Il Duomo*, parce qu'entre les deux niveaux du toit en courbe, vous vous retrouvez dans le vide. Vous êtes à l'intérieur même de la résistance du vide et vous en faites l'expérience, vous vous déplacez dedans. Cela a été l'élément fondateur de mon travail, de mon approche de l'ingénierie. C'est l'expérience du vide la plus importante qu'il m'ait été donné de vivre. C'est là qu'est née l'histoire de la passerelle Solférino : sur cette passerelle, vous allez d'un point à un autre à travers le vide. Je ne sais pas pourquoi je n'en ai jamais parlé avant. C'est pourtant la notion clé si l'on veut comprendre ma pratique de l'ingénierie. Vous êtes dans le vide ; vous passez à travers comme si vous ouvriez une fenêtre donnant sur le ciel. Vous avez une fenêtre entre les deux arches qui vous connecte au ciel. L'idée de pesanteur est profondément liée à cette idée de négocier notre relation au vide. C'est quelque chose de vraiment primordial : non seulement je ne l'ai jamais évoquée auparavant, mais je n'avais jusqu'ici jamais fait le lien avec le Dieu des Juifs.

JA Je suis content, nous en venons au sujet le plus important de cette conversation.

EA Pour développer des idées comme celle-ci, il faut du temps, non seulement verbalement, mais aussi par le biais de l'interaction entre le langage et l'image qui est la raison d'être de notre collaboration. Lors de mes premières visites du bâtiment Airtime, j'étais aussi fascinée par la structure et par la façon dont elle réencadrait le contexte. Je pense que pour Marc comme pour moi, il est essentiel de regarder en même temps à travers la structure et à l'intérieur de la structure. Parce que cette « machine à voir » ne devrait pas servir uniquement à regarder dehors ; elle devrait aussi amplifier ce sentiment d'être à l'intérieur de la structure ; c'est ce qui définit notre expérience de la ville. Je crois aussi que c'est ce que Marc entend et exprime quand il parle de « vide ».

MM Soyons honnêtes : l'architecture revient à cacher et à montrer. Vous voyez ce que l'architecte veut montrer et vous pouvez soit comprendre, soit ne pas comprendre ce que vous voyez. Vous devez donc choisir ce que vous voulez montrer ou ne pas montrer. Je m'inscris de toute évidence dans cette culture qui consiste à montrer. Mais montrer ne signifie pas forcément exposer les « muscles » ou le squelette du bâtiment. Pour moi, ce qui compte plus, c'est la cohérence urbaine de l'avenue de France. Je pense qu'il n'était pas nécessaire d'en faire trop, ni de cacher la structure, mais qu'il fallait plutôt ressentir cette structure, être relié au paysage. Cela apparaît dans la première étape du vocabulaire structurel et cela rend la lecture du projet un peu nébuleuse. Les éléments invisibles sont tout aussi importants que les éléments visibles.

JA Et toi, Erieta, quelle est ton approche du sujet? Que penses-tu de cette idée de révéler les qualités d'une architecture qui ne sont pas vraiment visibles?

EA Pour moi, l'essence même de la photographie est de révéler des qualités qui ne sont pas visibles au premier regard, qui doivent plutôt être débusquées. Bien sûr, on peut arriver devant un bâtiment et prendre plaisir à ce que l'on voit en surface. Mais si l'on va un peu plus loin, en particulier quand on visite un véritable complexe architectural, on commence à voir des choses que notre culture visuelle a du mal à saisir. Il y a tant de niveaux différents, qui exigeront souvent une approche narrative par le biais d'une série de photos qui dialogueront entre elles. Quelques images visuellement frappantes mais isolées ne peuvent pas saisir la complexité des transitions diurnes, saisonnières et même sociales. Ma mission consiste à rechercher ces éléments que nous ne sommes pas entraînés à voir. C'est pourquoi je passe des heures, et même des jours, sur place. C'est la seule façon de pouvoir repérer les nuances de l'interaction entre le bâtiment et son environnement à la fois physique et humain. Le bâtiment se révèle avec le temps. Tous les éléments se mettent en place à condition de prendre le temps nécessaire pour comprendre les interactions invisibles qui constituent l'architecture.

MM Erieta, quand tu découvres quelque chose de caché, est-ce que tu insistes dessus ou est-ce que tu le laisses tel quel?

EA Bien sûr que j'insiste; quel serait l'intérêt de laisser une chose cachée? Je la traite comme une cible. Chacun peut interpréter une image à sa façon et on ne peut pas échapper à la subjectivité, mais une intention, une intention consciente et déterminée, peut faire une différence qui se communique à travers l'image. C'est aussi pourquoi j'essaie toujours d'aller au-delà de la simple documentation.

JA Il y a aussi l'élément «temps» comme dimension de l'architecture. Il me semble très important d'enregistrer les différentes étapes de la construction comme tu l'as fait. Parce que le site de construction est le lieu principal de la narration architecturale: vous comprenez comment le bâtiment est créé. Et il me semble qu'une fois le bâtiment construit, vous gardez à l'esprit l'histoire de sa construction, qui peut être soit visible, soit cachée; l'architecture raconte en un sens l'histoire du bâtiment.

MM La construction n'est pas une phase: la construction est le bâtiment. Quand je regarde des photos d'architecture, je remarque souvent que les gens en sont absents. Or, cela m'intéresse beaucoup de voir comment les gens se déplacent parce que le bâtiment a été bâti avec «de la sueur et des larmes». Je veux que le public le sache. Le bâtiment est une mémoire de cette période: le projet est, avant tout, un processus. Il y a ici deux dimensions: l'une matérielle et l'autre humaine. La première consiste à montrer ce que l'on ne verra plus jamais, comme les lignes de chemin de fer non recouvertes ou les éléments structurels exposés. Même si vous percevez ces éléments dans la structure finale, vous ne les verrez pas de la même façon. La seconde dimension, c'est l'idée du bâtiment comme mémoire à travers les gens qui l'ont édifié. Ce souvenir est ce qui relie fondamentalement le bâtiment à la Terre puisque nous faisons partie de cet environnement plus large. Un bâtiment ne se matérialise pas en un instant. Et je veux comprendre et communiquer le processus de cette apparition. C'est pourquoi les images d'Erieta m'intéressent : elles montrent la lourdeur, beaucoup de structure, beaucoup d'acier, beaucoup de gens travaillant sur le site. Ces éléments qui vont disparaître, mais définissent néanmoins l'identité finale du bâtiment, sont présents dans ses images. Je suis très heureux qu'elle ait pu les prendre.

EA Même moi, quand je me penche à nouveau sur les premières photos prises il y a deux ans, je ressens leur légitimité et ce sentiment d'accomplissement. Je suis si contente qu'on les ait faites. C'est la confirmation de l'importance qu'il y avait à être présent, à se lancer dans le projet et à suivre les moindres changements et transitions de la structure. Je me rendais sur le site au moins une fois tous les deux mois. Quand je photographiais Airtime, j'essayais toujours de garder à l'esprit l'idée d'un pont. Mais ensuite, Marc m'a dit que le pont ne serait pas important car il serait recouvert. À partir de là, c'est ce que j'ai décidé de vraiment essayer de montrer; je ne voulais pas seulement le montrer une fois, je voulais essayer de le capturer systématiquement à travers l'évolution de la structure et la façon dont elle recadre les paysages alentour et leur donne une nouvelle forme. D'une certaine façon, il s'agit de la propre histoire de Marc et de ce qu'il nous transmet: le site tout au long du processus de développement avant qu'il ne soit totalement recouvert, et la zone avant que le pont ne devienne un «faux terrain». Par nécessité, je dois comprendre la vision de Marc avec les outils de mon propre langage. Donc, pendant que la structure s'élève, je ne peux vraiment pas m'empêcher de voir le pont, les ouvriers dessus et les trains qui accélèrent dessous. C'est quelque chose dont vous ne pourrez plus faire l'expérience dans environ deux ans mais cela fait néanmoins partie de l'identité du bâtiment.

JA Je me demande si tu n'abordes pas ici aussi un autre aspect, un aspect sociopolitique: si la valeur et la richesse reposent sur le travail en tant que tel, cela signifie que vous êtes profondément attachés à combattre la dévaluation de ce travail. De nos jours, le travail physique est très dévalué et vous nous rappelez que la réalité même de la valeur repose sur le travail. Est-ce que vous diriez tous les deux que c'est une notion importante pour vous?

MM Oui, n'oubliez pas que mon père était tailleur. Je me souviens qu'enfant, je voyais des gens regarder les tissus, les couper et tracer des patrons. Quand vous appliquez un patron sur un tissu, vous le faites de manière à gâcher le moins de tissu possible au moment de la coupe. Mon père pouvait venir me voir et me dire: «Marc, cette épaule est mal faite.» Tout comptait: les matériaux, le travail nécessaire pour leur donner forme, les procédés qui permettaient d'éviter le gaspillage grâce à l'efficacité. Finalement c'est ce que nous faisons avec l'acier, depuis les détails jusqu'à l'ensemble, puisque les matériaux font le lien entre les deux. Quand j'accueille quelqu'un et que je lui demande comment il va, je m'attache instinctivement aux tissus qu'il ou elle porte, comme mon père le faisait. Il touchait les tissus pour voir comment ils réagissaient sous ses doigts, simplement pour comprendre s'il s'agissait de soie, de laine ou d'une autre fibre. Avoir ce rapport à la matérialité des choses était important.

EA Je me souviens d'un séjour à Tokyo avec Marc, pendant lequel nous sommes entrés dans plusieurs boutiques de vêtements. Il se mettait toujours à tout toucher, pas seulement les produits exposés mais aussi les murs et les surfaces. Il scannait tout du regard pour essayer de comprendre les matériaux et les formes. C'était passionnant d'assister à cela en direct et d'avoir ainsi un aperçu de la façon dont il approche l'architecture.

MM Mais mes mains font aussi partie de mes yeux.

JA Erieta, tu as aussi un rapport visuel à la texture.

EA Oui, quand j'étais photographe d'archéologie, mon travail consistait en partie à révéler les textures. C'était un processus essentiel, lié à l'identification et la documentation scientifiques des découvertes. Je m'intéressais tout particulièrement aux peintures murales, aux murs et aux surfaces architecturales dans les tombes de l'Antiquité, ainsi qu'aux microsculptures et aux objets en ivoire trouvés sous terre. J'essayais de donner à voir toutes les textures et formes de ces minuscules artefacts et ce n'était pas facile. On m'apportait des chariots contenant environ 200 objets et je devais les mettre en valeur un par un. Cette méthode de travail a survécu dans ma photo d'architecture avec la révélation de la texture.

MM Comment es-tu passée des objets archéologiques de petite échelle aux paysages ?

EA Les fragments archéologiques sont en réalité des restes d'objets du quotidien et de bâtiments dispersés sur un site mais en fait intimement reliés les uns aux autres. Une partie du travail archéologique consiste à essayer de comprendre l'image d'ensemble que ces restes forment et c'est en révélant leur relation au contexte général qu'on peut le faire. Dans mon travail, j'ai donc commencé à m'intéresser à des sites archéologiques dans leur intégralité, où ce qui reliait entre eux les fragments architecturaux érodés était le paysage lui-même. Je devais donc aussi photographier ce paysage. C'était inévitable. J'ai photographié l'intégralité du site de fouilles de Cnossos en Crète – une de mes plus grosses commandes. Ce travail a une importance particulière pour moi, en partie aussi à cause de l'époque à laquelle je l'ai réalisé. C'était juste après mon premier long séjour au Japon : j'avais sillonné le pays pendant cinq mois pour photographier l'architecture contemporaine en verre. Le contraste entre le verre dans un contexte très avant-gardiste et un palais en pierre vieux de 3 000 ans est très intrigant et cela a remis en question tout mon appareillage conceptuel en tant que photographe. Il s'agissait à chaque fois de paysages peuplés de fragments architecturaux mais ils se manifestaient de façon totalement différente.

MM De toute évidence, l'archéologie a trait à la mémoire, mais tu parles aussi de mémoire dans ton travail contemporain.

EA Oui, la mémoire opère à différentes échelles et c'est aussi quelque chose que j'ai entrevu pour la première fois au Japon et à Cnossos il y a vingt ans. Je suis passée d'un environnement architectural en verre presque abstrait au sein du paysage japonais à un site de fouilles archéologiques en pleine activité où je photographiais méticuleusement mur par mur, millimètre par millimètre, chaque infime trace avec une précision scientifique. Il s'agissait de deux façons totalement différentes d'approcher des structures créées par l'homme et de prendre en compte les souvenirs encodés en elles. D'un côté, vous avez des strates de verre dont les réflexions compriment paysage et architecture en une seule entité ; elles les entremêlent et créent cette narration où contenu et contexte sont imbriqués. De l'autre côté, vous avez de véritables strates de matériaux, solidifiées les unes sur les autres après des siècles passés sous terre ; un récit archéologique, presque un journal intime de ces transitions, est inscrit dans la texture même de ces murs.

MM C'est là où je veux en venir. La mémoire est inscrite dans l'archéologie et tu as commencé par ça, mais tu es peut-être d'autant plus intéressée par la mémoire dans l'architecture contemporaine que tu as auparavant travaillé avec le prisme archéologique.

EA C'est possible, mais la mémoire fait partie intégrante de l'expérience de l'architecture, et ce, quelle que soit la période. Quand j'ai photographié le pavillon de verre de Kengo Kuma and Associates à New Canaan, dans le Connecticut, je l'ai fait sur une période de deux ans et à des saisons différentes. Le passage d'une saison à l'autre, et la façon dont ce passage modifie notre perception de l'espace, est lié à l'idée que l'espace inscrit continuellement des souvenirs en lui-même par le biais d'une interaction avec le contexte. L'espace est une expérience à plusieurs strates : c'est beaucoup plus que l'apparence extérieure d'un bâtiment ou son image. Il y a un équilibre fragile entre la structure, l'environnement naturel et les phénomènes lumineux et climatiques – toujours en évolution.

MM La fragilité, c'est bien de cela qu'il s'agit : la fragilité que nous percevons quand nous observons la Terre, les paysages. C'est ce que j'essaie de faire : négocier cet équilibre fragile. Et il y a un mot que je n'utilise jamais mais qui ne cesse de revenir dans les questions qu'on me pose, c'est le mot « intégration ». Beaucoup de gens me demandent si j'ai la possibilité ou l'ambition d'intégrer mon projet au paysage. Je leur réponds toujours : « Comment voulez-vous intégrer un pont au beau milieu d'une vallée ? » Imaginez que vous éleviez un pont d'une colline à une autre : c'est un acte d'agression envers le paysage, et le mieux que nous puissions faire, c'est de tenter de créer un dialogue avec le paysage. C'est un équilibre difficile. Erieta le sait, elle prend l'aspect éphémère du paysage comme point de départ et explore l'interface avec les constructions, avec l'architecture et son image. Et puisqu'on parle d'image, je pense que c'est également lié à l'idée de style architectural. Le style n'a absolument aucune signification s'il est déconnecté de tous les thèmes que nous venons d'aborder. L'architecture n'est pas un accessoire de mode.

JA Je ne pense pas que le mot « style » soit un terme utile ; ce qui est plus important, c'est la manière dont vous donnez forme. Je voudrais savoir si Erieta, quand elle fait ce genre d'images, s'attache à cette expression de l'architecture, de la forme particulière.

EA Le bâtiment parle pour lui-même ; en fait, c'est lui qui dicte d'une certaine façon la séance photo. La forme est un facteur essentiel dans la mesure où elle révèle certaines qualités de l'architecture, mais c'est le cas aussi des conditions lumineuses qui sont souvent liées à une zone géographique particulière. J'essaie en général de souligner certains aspects d'un bâtiment de façon à révéler des réalités en présence dans la plupart des œuvres architecturales. C'est un mécanisme de pensée qui va du particulier à l'universel. Mais bien sûr, ça ne marche pas toujours pour tout le monde. Dans le cas de l'architecture de Marc, c'est extrêmement bien défini : la lumière du soleil joue un grand rôle dans beaucoup de ses bâtiments, alors que dans d'autres, comme Airtime, le temps nuageux attire notre attention sur le contexte. Il révèle ces connexions.

JA J'ai une question sur la façon dont tu ressens tes propres photographies. Je vois d'abord la réaction des matériaux, des surfaces, et le mouvement de la lumière par le biais de la réflexion. Quelque chose dans l'architecture fait écho à la façon dont la lumière est saisie. Quel est le lien entre cette réflexion de la lumière et la façon dont tu pénètres visuellement dans le bâtiment, dont tu en découvres l'intérieur ?

EA À chaque œuvre architecturale correspond un type de lumière différent qui révélera ses caractéristiques intrinsèques ; tout dépend de la forme et du matériau, et plus encore du contexte. Par exemple, à Roland-Garros, nous avons besoin de soleil, sinon nous aurons une lecture du lieu complètement différente qui révèlera peut-être d'autres aspects mais pas les plus importants. Mon sentiment, c'est que Marc l'a conçu, peut-être inconsciemment, comme un bâtiment dont il faut faire l'expérience en plein soleil. Quand je commence à observer un site, je sais quel type de lumière sera idéal mais parfois je n'ai pas le choix ; là j'ai eu la chance d'avoir le choix. Ceci dit, ce qui compte encore plus, c'est qu'avec le travail de Marc, nous avons toujours le choix grâce à cette collaboration à long terme que nous avons établie. À quelques exceptions près, nous pouvons revisiter et repenser le travail ensemble. Parfois, comme au Maroc, nous n'avons pas eu le choix mais nous avons eu la chance d'avoir la lumière dont nous avions besoin. Donc, encore une fois, vous pouvez voir que plus que la forme, c'est la lumière que je tente de suivre. En tant que photographe, la lumière me fournit les outils pour dialoguer avec la création architecturale, ses effets et ses intentions. La forme arrive pour ainsi dire après coup.

MM Oui, c'est un sujet compliqué. Après tout, la forme est la qualité la plus importante, la plus objective, de l'architecture. Mais la forme, c'est comme l'amour : vous ne pouvez pas en parler vous-même puisque c'est le résultat de tout le processus dont nous sommes en train de parler. Elle naît du jeu entre la matérialité, la mémoire et le paysage. Ces trois notions s'adressent à nous continuellement et nous devons être à leur écoute. Le site est très important, c'est pourquoi je dis toujours à mes étudiants : « Vous devez écouter le lieu, vous devez ressentir la situation que vous produisez par le biais de votre création. » On fait un projet pour entamer un dialogue, on le fait évoluer tandis que le dialogue s'enrichit. Et le dialogue est un processus horizontal – non pas hiérarchique, mais réciproque et continu. À l'opposé pour ainsi dire de l'analyse qui, elle, est une approche verticale. Je n'utilise jamais ce mot, « analyse ». Quand j'étais étudiant, nous devions souvent faire des analyses de sites afin de développer nos projets. Cela n'a aucun sens pour moi, c'est hors sujet. L'analyse n'a aucun sens en architecture, le projet est en soi une analyse. Le projet réagira d'une certaine façon à une situation et exprimera cette réaction sous forme bâtie. C'est ce que nous devrions aborder quand nous parlons de style, ou de forme. Et Erieta comprend très bien cela, ce processus continu de dialogue qui est très différent de l'analyse verticale.

JA C'est d'ailleurs au cœur de cette collaboration entre l'architecte et le photographe : c'est l'objet principal de cet ouvrage et son format.

EA Exactement. Je voudrais insister sur le rôle qu'a joué Marc, car en me donnant la possibilité d'opérer selon mes propres termes, il a permis que tout ceci se produise. Ce projet ne se serait jamais fait sans que Marc s'autorise lui-même à explorer de nouvelles façons de dialoguer à la fois avec l'architecture et avec le paysage. Cela vaut la peine de mentionner comment cette collaboration est née, ce que Marc a vu dans mon travail photographique, ce qui lui a donné envie de se lancer dans ce projet. Moi, j'ai repéré une connexion dès le tout début, quand j'ai assisté à l'une de ses conférences. Mais c'est à sa décision et non à la mienne que l'on doit ce projet. C'était fascinant car le fait qu'un architecte ou un ingénieur réalise le potentiel d'une telle collaboration signifie que son mécanisme de pensée opère en dehors de la stricte approche technique traditionnelle. Les architectes font en général appel à un photographe pour des raisons purement documentaires et cela n'a aucun potentiel pour moi. Marc s'est mis peu à peu, étape par étape, à me laisser faire ce que je voulais. Plus il voyait mon travail, plus il découvrait des choses à propos de lui-même et de son architecture qu'il trouvait intéressantes de me voir développer. Notre collaboration s'apparentait même à une sorte de « métadialogue » sur des dialogues qui ont lieu à la fois en architecture et en photographie : une longueur d'avance, deux longueurs d'avance, un pas en arrière, un pas en avant, afin de révéler toutes ces différentes histoires. Donc cela n'a pas été tout de suite évident et cela s'est développé sur un certain temps. Marc découvrait les résultats au fur et à mesure, il s'en emparait, travaillait dessus ; il ne faisait pas que réagir aux photos, il laissait les idées mûrir en lui. Cela a pris évidemment du temps. Je suis peut-être quelqu'un de très expérimenté du point de vue du langage visuel photographique, je sais ce que je recherche et comment l'articuler, mais Marc, en tant qu'ingénieur, utilise un vocabulaire différent et des outils intellectuels différents dans son appréhension de l'espace. Nous avions besoin de nous adonner à une sorte de traduction visuelle ; c'est ce que nous avons fait et c'est là que le véritable dialogue a commencé.

MM La première fois que j'ai été en contact avec la photographie d'Erieta – et bien sûr après en avoir parlé avec elle, puisque nous ne sommes pas entraînés à voir l'intentionnalité dans une photographie et que nous ne voyons en général que les formes ou l'image –, j'ai été très intrigué par deux notions : la matérialité et les limites. Les images d'Erieta reposent beaucoup sur l'idée que la texture peut communiquer visuellement une réalité matérielle ; ensuite, la photographie elle-même, selon le type de support sur laquelle elle est imprimée, peut ajouter un deuxième niveau de texture sur l'image, ce qui affecte la façon dont nous l'appréhendons. Et Erieta utilise cela pour transformer l'image de la construction en une conversation – entre la construction et tout le reste, y compris celui ou celle qui regarde la photographie. Engager le dialogue avec la matérialité est une façon de donner un sens à la transformation de la Terre. L'architecture, je l'ai déjà dit, est un art de la transformation ; on prend le monde, on le transforme en matériaux, on transforme les matériaux en construction et la construction en une nouvelle matérialité. Cette relation que nous avons avec la planète est absolument centrale dans ma conception de l'architecture, et les images d'Erieta font toujours référence à ce point. La façon dont vous lisez le paysage définit la façon dont vous lisez la transformation de la Terre. Et puis, en étroite relation avec ce que nous venons de dire, vous avez l'idée de limite : les limites entre les choses, et la façon dont la photographie peut les souligner, les amoindrir ou les mélanger. L'idée qu'il ne s'agisse pas seulement d'un jeu de mots me fascine : travailler « dans les limites », « à la limite », est aussi l'essence de mon rôle en tant qu'ingénieur. J'essaie de déceler la limite du poids, la limite de la portée, la limite du matériau, et Erieta se retrouve toujours en équilibre à la limite du monde, à la limite du sol. Voilà, c'est l'idée de la périphérie, de la limite. Donc si on prend en compte ces deux notions – matérialité et limite –, on comprend qu'elles peuvent être appliquées à tout ce qui constitue notre environnement : le paysage ou encore une maison en verre.

EA C'est une leçon qu'on apprend quand on dialogue avec l'archéologie : on capture les transformations à la fois matérielles et atmosphériques par le biais de leurs transitions ou de leurs limites.

JA C'est essentiel puisque vous devez vous confronter à l'invisible avec les moyens de la visibilité. Et nous avons parlé de ce qui est visible et de ce qui ne l'est pas.

MM C'est une notion centrale dans la discipline architecturale et en particulier dans l'univers de la structure : décider de ce qui doit être montré et de ce qui doit être dissimulé. Pour revenir aux deux notions de matérialité et de limite, Erieta regarde quelque chose que tout le monde voit mais que personne ne peut voir comme elle le voit, avec ses yeux. Donc elle donne un sens à quelque chose qui pourrait passer inaperçu pour l'observateur lambda en l'intégrant dans un récit plus large ; elle place cette chose dans un contexte ; elle recrée et interprète le paysage en face de nous. Je suis particulièrement fasciné par l'idée que la photographie – comme tout autre système, d'ailleurs, mais c'est de photographie dont nous parlons aujourd'hui – peut être abordée par le biais de sa capacité à révéler le sens des choses. Et ce que j'essaie de faire – à travers mon travail –, c'est ce qu'Erieta fait. Nous en sommes donc arrivés à un point où elle révèle avec ses moyens ce que j'essaie de faire avec les miens. Elle dispose une couche de pensée sur la couche d'architecture. Et pour couronner le tout, elle le fait avec un appareil argentique. C'est un peu fou, cette obsession pour la texture et la matérialité qui s'étend à la matérialité même du produit final sur papier.

EA Non seulement c'est un appareil argentique, mais c'est un grand format 10 × 12 centimètres avec un dos panoramique. Je photographie en format paysage puisque pour moi toute architecture est un paysage. Le format large et horizontal, ce n'est pas juste pour moi une obsession esthétique. Même quand j'ai un objet carré devant moi, je le photographie en format panoramique car il y a toujours cette idée sous-jacente de continuité du paysage ; le paysage rassemble tout. Dans un autre contexte de travail, vous pouvez prendre des instantanés, mais ici ce n'est tout simplement pas possible ; ce genre de pratique ne l'autorise pas. Un exemple : en septembre 2016, j'ai vu le site d'Airtime pour la première fois, et c'était le premier bâtiment de Marc que je photographiais. À cette époque, il n'y avait bien sûr rien d'autre qu'une dalle. Mais dès ce moment, parce que le travail de Marc m'intéressait, j'ai été très intriguée par le site. Il pleuvait et il y avait des nuages le premier jour – un temps typiquement parisien –, avec cette lumière diffuse blanchâtre. On pouvait voir les trains passer et le nouveau bâtiment s'élever lentement. J'ai essayé de visualiser la façon dont le dialogue se créerait entre le contexte environnant et l'architecture encore en devenir. Les architectes ont une vision toujours extrêmement précise et détaillée de leurs bâtiments car ils ont en tête à la fois le bâtiment et le séquencement de sa construction. Mais dans mon cas, en tant qu'élément étranger, il me fallait bâtir cette vision de zéro en ne m'appuyant que sur le site en évolution. En conséquence, plus je le voyais s'élever et se connecter avec la ville de différentes façons, plus je voulais comprendre et expliquer ce lieu spécifique qui est en quelque sorte le générateur des idées de Marc.

JA Erieta, est-ce que tu peux nous en dire plus sur la distance, la distance spatiale, que tu adoptes avec tes sujets ? Je suis frappé de constater que la plupart de tes images sont prises de loin et qu'il n'y a presque jamais de gros plans.

EA Je ne crois pas aux photos prises de près sauf dans des situations très particulières. Ce qui m'intéresse, c'est l'inversion entre contenu et contexte, la mise à plat des hiérarchies entre les objets et leur environnement, et pour cela, il faut se mettre à distance de l'objet. Sinon, si vous vous approchez de trop près, la relation avec le contexte va vous échapper ; vous allez l'amputer. Vous allez certes peut-être révéler des détails, mais jamais de connexions, et c'est justement ce qui m'intéresse. Cette approche qui consiste à étudier l'architecture par le biais de détails visuels jette la confusion dans la photographie d'architecture car elle encourage le fétichisme de la composition visuelle et donne en conséquence la priorité à l'objet et à la forme. Une telle approche n'aurait jamais fonctionné avec l'architecture de Marc parce qu'elle exige que l'horizon et la lumière puissent avoir leur place et que l'intérieur et l'extérieur fusionnent.

MM Vous voyez, même le vocabulaire qu'elle utilise est le même que celui que j'utilise. Je vous ai déjà dit que j'étais presque plus impressionné par les architectes paysagistes que par les architectes. À cause de ce travail en dialogue avec l'horizon, et aussi du fait de cette relation à la Terre, du format panoramique. C'est exactement ce que j'essaie de faire dans mon travail. La semaine dernière, je devais aller en Allemagne étudier un paysage pour un concours que nous faisons là-bas, et je me disais : « Mais pourquoi est-ce que je vais sur place ? » Après tout, j'ai Google, ça devrait suffire. Puis je me suis repris : je dis à tout le monde, à mes étudiants, qu'on doit toujours aller sur le site, et moi-même je ne vais pas y aller ? Alors j'ai fait mon sac, j'y suis allé et j'ai vécu une belle expérience. Parce que vous ressentez l'endroit, et vous ressentez le terrain et la Terre. Nous marchons sur le terrain et nous érigeons depuis le terrain : l'idée de bâtiment est donc pour moi similaire à celle d'un homme qui se coucherait puis se relèverait ; l'architecture est une relation à la pesanteur. C'est une relation exceptionnelle à la pesanteur et on ne peut pas s'en dispenser.

JA Il y a cette expression en français, « la réalité du terrain »... Dans ton cas, il semblerait que tu aies atteint cette réalité du terrain. C'est essentiel car c'est la clé si nous voulons comprendre le contexte.

MM Toute construction existe en relation avec le terrain. Airtime est le seul bâtiment qui mette en valeur la différence entre le vrai sol et le faux sol ; la façon dont un bâtiment repose sur le terrain est ce qui fait fusionner l'architecture avec son contexte. Tout commence au niveau du terrain et se prolonge vers le ciel ; il n'y a pas d'architecture flottante. Ça n'existe pas. J'aime bien l'expression en anglais « good ground », une bonne base, un bon terrain. Cette idée que nous sommes connectés au terrain selon la formule $g = 9{,}81\,m/s^2$ est très importante, et nous ne pouvons pas nous permettre de l'oublier car toute notre relation au terrain est fondée sur cela. C'est ce qu'Erieta révèle à sa façon, et c'est ce que j'essaie de voir à ma façon à travers ses photographies. C'est la première fois que je me lance dans une telle introspection avec un photographe, et peut-être la dernière !

Biographie de Marc Mimram
Architecte ingénieur | → p. 86

Né à Paris en 1955, Marc Mimram est titulaire d'une maîtrise en mathématiques de l'université Paris VII (1976), d'un diplôme d'ingénieur de l'École nationale des ponts et chaussées (1978), d'une maîtrise en génie civil de l'université de Californie à Berkeley (1979) et d'un diplôme d'architecture (DPLG) de l'École nationale supérieure des beaux-arts de Paris (1980).
Depuis 1992, il développe au sein d'une même structure une double activité d'architecte et d'ingénieur.
À partir de 1981, date à laquelle il débute comme architecte ingénieur, il réalise de nombreux ouvrages d'art et projets architecturaux en France et à l'étranger : des ponts en France (comme la passerelle Solférino à Paris), en Allemagne (avec la liaison Strasbourg-Kehl), en Chine (à Pékin, Tianjin et Yangzhou) ou encore au Maroc (entre Rabat et Salé), ce dernier projet ayant remporté le Prix Aga Khan, ainsi que des bâtiments tels que de grandes installations sportives (stade Roland-Garros, piscines, etc.) et des infrastructures (comme le bâtiment Airtime à Paris ou la gare de Montpellier).
Marc Mimram a enseigné à l'École des ponts et chaussées à Paris, à l'École polytechnique fédérale de Lausanne et à l'université de Princeton aux États-Unis. Il a été nommé professeur des écoles nationales supérieures d'architecture et enseigne actuellement à l'école d'architecture de Marne-la-Vallée, près de Paris.
Il a publié différents ouvrages de réflexion sur sa discipline et son travail. Citons par exemple *Structure et formes* (Paris, Dunod, 1983), *Marc Mimram, Passerelle Solférino* (Bâle, 2001), *Architettura Ibrida* (Milan, Electa Architettura, 2009), *Marc Mimram, Architecture et structure* (Munich, Prestel, 2015).
Dans le cadre de conférences, il intervient en outre dans le monde entier (Harvard, Cornell, Princeton, Tokyo, São Paulo, Venise, Oslo, etc.).

Dans son travail d'architecte et d'ingénieur, Marc Mimram démontre un intérêt pour une architecture intelligemment construite à travers le développement de structures réfléchies qui se rapportent au paysage, à la lumière et aux matériaux. Il conçoit son travail comme une transformation attentive et généreuse de la matière dont le monde est fait. Entre ses mains, l'architecture devient un art de la transformation, et la matérialité une expression sensible de la culture.

Biographie d'Erieta Attali
Photographe de paysage et d'architecture | → p. 87

Née à Tel Aviv, Erieta Attali a grandi à Istanbul, puis Athènes. Elle vit actuellement entre New York et Paris et photographie le travail d'architectes contemporains à travers le monde. Elle a commencé sa carrière en 1993 en tant que photographe de paysage et d'archéologie, s'intéressant plus particulièrement aux sites funéraires souterrains. Depuis vingt ans, elle se consacre avant tout à la photographie de paysage et d'architecture aussi bien en Europe que sur le continent américain, en Asie ou en Australie. Ses travaux commandités par des institutions publiques ou universitaires ont fait l'objet de plusieurs expositions et monographies. Son œuvre fait partie de la collection permanente de la National Gallery of Victoria (NGV) de Melbourne. Diplômée en photographie du Goldsmiths College de l'université de Londres, Erieta Attali a ensuite poursuivi ses études à la School of Architecture, Planning & Preservation (GSAPP) de l'université de Columbia à New York grâce au soutien de la Fulbright Foundation, ainsi qu'à l'université Waseda de Tokyo avec le concours de la Japan Foundation. Elle est également titulaire d'un doctorat de la School of Architecture & Design de la RMIT University de Melbourne. Entre 2003 et 2018, Erieta Attali a enseigné la photographie d'architecture à la GSAPP de Columbia. Elle a été professeur invitée à la faculté d'architecture de l'université technique de Munich (TUM), à l'école d'architecture de l'université catholique du Chili, à l'Académie royale des beaux-arts du Danemark à Copenhague, à l'Architectural Association à Londres, à la RMIT à Melbourne, à l'université de Tokyo, à Technion à Haïfa en Israël ou encore à l'université de Sydney. Erieta Attali effectue actuellement un travail de recherche au sein de l'Académie d'architecture à Paris. Elle est également artiste en résidence à la Cité internationale des arts où elle mène un projet photographique sur Paris et la Seine. Elle a écrit et édité de nombreux ouvrages parmi lesquels on compte *Glass | Wood*, *Erieta Attali on Kengo Kuma* et *Periphery | Archaeology of Light*, publiés par les éditions Hatje Cantz.

Biographie de Jean Attali | → p. 88

Jean Attali est professeur émérite à l'École nationale supérieure d'architecture Paris-Malaquais. Philosophe, il consacre depuis de nombreuses années ses écrits, son enseignement et ses recherches à l'architecture et à l'urbanisme. De 2007 à 2016, il a dirigé un séminaire de recherche consacré à un « atlas partagé » du paysage urbain mondial, disponible en ligne et bientôt sous forme de livre. Il a publié un grand nombre de textes aussi bien dans le domaine de l'architecture que dans celui de la géographie urbaine, de l'urbanisme, de l'art contemporain et de la photographie. Parmi ses ouvrages, citons *Le Plan et le Détail. Une philosophie de l'architecture et de la ville* (Nîmes, 2001), *Retours de mer* (Paris, 2014) et *Elements Europa. European Council and Council of the European Union* avec Philippe Samyn (Bruxelles, 2016).

Remerciements de Marc Mimram | → p. 102

Je tiens à exprimer toute ma gratitude envers AG2R La Mondiale pour son soutien et Isabelle Clerc pour son appui et sa patience.
Ma reconnaissance va à Icade et Emmanuelle Baboulin qui m'a fait confiance dans le développement d'un projet innovant technologiquement, structurellement et en modes d'usages. La prise de risque est une qualité de la maîtrise d'ouvrage.

Ce livre est le fruit d'une rencontre entre le regard sensible et exigeant d'Erieta Attali et nos convictions construites ; je la remercie pour cette attention, cette détermination sans limite.

L'architecture se représente le plus souvent dans ses atours resplendissants, sous des cieux tropicaux quelle que soit leur situation, parés du maquillage informatisé de transformismes éclatants.
Difficile de créer une émotion, de refléter une atmosphère, d'exprimer une matérialité tant les codes de la représentation photoshopée abandonnent le réel pour plonger dans une virtualité virtuose mais délétère, mortifère, alors que notre engagement porte générosité et sensibilité au monde.

La rencontre avec la photographe Erieta Attali a permis de sortir de cette course à la « fake representation » qui, comme la « fake news », ne serait pas un mensonge mais une interprétation du réel.
Erieta Attali a depuis trois ans mis ses pas dans ceux de nos chantiers, glissant son regard dans l'objectif de son appareil. L'objectif est subjectif, le travail d'interprétation est toujours présent, et pourtant la photographe construit ici une mixité qui n'est pas stylistique, mais s'inscrit dans une figuration de l'architecture sensible et émotionnelle. Les reflets matérialisés des lumières, les textures et le grain de la peau ou la massivité prolongent un travail disciplinaire tant sur l'architecture que sur la facture de celle-ci. Entre l'éphémère du chantier et la permanence apparente des enjeux construits, Erieta Attali aura porté son regard sur les chantiers en cours, les projets construits d'ouvrages d'art ou de bâtiments, pour montrer qu'au-delà d'un style affirmé et délocalisé, il s'agit bien d'une démarche cohérente, engagée.

J'apprécie sans réserve sa disponibilité et ses qualités d'abnégation. Cette quête est rare, je souhaitais ici la souligner.

Ce projet a fait l'objet de développements attentifs, aussi bien par les architectes que les ingénieurs qui y ont collaboré. L' équipe de projet a été nombreuse tant au sein de Marc Mimram Architecture & Associés que Marc Mimram Ingénierie. Je les remercie pour leur engagement, et particulièrement Guillaume André, Martin Fougeras Lavergnolle, Razvan Ionica, Liu Chengyin et Anne-Marie De Matos.

Le projet est la mémoire du travail de tous ceux qui ont donné courage et intelligence, souvent dans l'anonymat. Qu'ils soient ici remerciés, car leur participation au projet est une matière à penser l'architecture. Les bâtiments, les ouvrages d'art réalisés forment la mémoire construite de notre travail partagé. Ouvriers ou ingénieurs, ils entreprennent au sens noble du mot, et le projet met ses espoirs en leur savoir.

KOMA AMOK, nos graphistes, ont montré une finesse dans l'interprétation graphique des photographies en résonance avec l'architecture des projets. Aris Kafantaris a été un indispensable ordonnateur.

Jean Attali a porté une contribution essentielle, tant dans l'écoute que dans la clarification exacte de nos échanges.

Remerciements d'Erieta Attali | → p. 103

Le 14 juillet 2016, j'ai eu la chance d'être invitée par Farrokh Derakshani, directeur du prix Aga Khan d'architecture, à « Beyond The Bridge », une conférence au Victoria & Albert Museum de Londres. Parmi les intervenants, j'ai remarqué le nom d'un homme, Marc Mimram. Je ne le connaissais pas mais sa courte biographie m'a donné envie de l'écouter parler de ses ponts. Avant la fin même de son intervention, j'ai su quel serait mon prochain projet : explorer ses infrastructures à travers la France et au-delà, ses ponts, ses gares et ses piscines.
Avant la conférence de Marc, j'avais déjà photographié des monuments, historiques ou contemporains, à travers le monde. Je venais juste de finir mes études doctorales en Australie et j'allais publier quelques monographies. Le timing était donc parfait : je pourrais mettre ma vision et mes désirs au service de cette nouvelle entreprise – un périple de trois ans à travers les réalisations et les créations sculpturales de Marc Mimram.

Je remercie Marc pour sa confiance. Il ne me l'a pas donnée d'emblée ; j'ai dû la gagner étape par étape et nous avons fini par atteindre une sorte d'apogée : l'achèvement d'une série d'études décodant le paysage par le biais de constructions infrastructurelles se déployant à travers les paysages, reliant et créant de nouvelles réalités pour le quotidien de tous. Pour moi, cela a aussi été un voyage au sens littéral du terme : des régions les plus reculées du monde où j'avais passé plus de deux décennies vers le cœur de Paris. Et puis je n'ai pas fait que capturer le monde de Marc ; j'ai eu la grande chance qu'il partage avec moi ses visions et ses rêves.

Merci Marc.

Je suis reconnaissante à tous les membres de l'agence Marc Mimram et en particulier à :
Anne-Marie De Matos, Marine Farouault, Cynthia Jupin,
Ignacio Olalquiaga Varela, et Liu Chengyin, Chine.

Je remercie les personnes suivantes qui m'ont aidée à différentes étapes de ce projet :

Chez Hatje Cantz :
Son ancien directeur, Holger Liebs, ainsi que Claire Cichy et toute l'équipe pour avoir cru en mon art et m'avoir soutenue tout au long de ce projet.
Tous les traducteurs et relecteurs :
Aaron Bogart, Caroline Higgit, Anne Levine, Isabelle Liber.

Mise en page :
Merci à KOMA AMOK, l'agence de graphisme de Stuttgart, pour son soutien inconditionnel et l'intensité exceptionnelle avec laquelle son équipe s'est plongée dans cette monographie complexe en trois volumes, traduisant ainsi mon regard photographique et la façon dont j'ai capturé l'ingénierie et l'architecture de Marc ; je les remercie pour leur conviction et leur amitié.
Le responsable éditorial des textes :
Merci à Aris Kafantaris, architecte et responsable éditorial basé à Tokyo, pour son soutien à toutes les étapes de la création de cette monographie, de la naissance de l'idée de ce livre à son impression.

Les auteurs des textes :
Jean Attali, Paul Chemetov, Sir Peter Cook, Ariel Genadt, Zvi Hecker.

Services photographiques et assistance :
DIGID'A Lab à Rome. Davide Di Gianni et Fabio Barile,
pour la qualité exceptionnelle de leurs services.
Assistants photographes :
Philipp Valente et Lukas Walcher, TUM University, Architecture ;
Daniel Raphael Zuvia, Graduate School of Architecture,
Planning & Preservation, Columbia University, NYC.
Assistance technique pour le volume III sur Roland-Garros :
Michel Ellert et Gilles Cargueray, Leica, France ;
Charles Plumey, Paris.

Et enfin, et surtout :
Mon respect éternel à Kleio & Kazim.

Acknowledgments of Marc Mimram

My warmest thanks to AG2R La Mondiale for its support and to Isabelle Clerc for her assistance and patience.
I am indebted to Icade and Emmanuelle Baboulin, who encouraged me in the development of a project that was innovative not only technologically and structurally but also in its modes of use. One of the qualities of project management is a readiness to take risks.

This book is the result of an encounter between the sensitive and demanding eye of Erieta Attali and our architectural belief. I thank her for this attention, this limitless determination.

Architecture is generally depicted in all its dazzling splendor beneath impossibly blue skies, dramatically transformed by digital manipulation. The rules of such Photoshopped creations depart so far from the truth in their search for virtuosic virtual reality that it is hard to create a mood, reflect an atmosphere, or express materiality. They damage and deaden where our collaboration seeks to bring generosity and sensitivity to the world.

Our meeting with the photographer Erieta Attali made it possible to turn away from the race to "fake representation" which, like "fake news," is not so much a lie as an interpretation of reality.
Erieta Attali has spent three years following our building projects, observing them through her photographic lens. The lens is subjective and interpretation is always present, but here the photographer has constructed an architecture through the senses and emotions. The materialized reflections of light, the textures of flesh, or the sensation of mass can all be found in her work whether dealing with architecture or the creation of architecture. Between the ever-changing aspect of a building site and the apparent permanence of the final construction, Erieta Attali has depicted both building sites and completed examples of civil engineering projects and buildings, demonstrating that beyond her distinctive and detached style lies a committed and coherent approach.

I am grateful for her generosity with her time and her selflessness. I cannot stress enough how rare these qualities are.

This project is the object of attentive development from both the collaborating architects and engineers. Many people have been involved in the project teams, Marc Mimram Architecture & Associés and Marc Mimram Ingénierie. My thanks go to them for their contributions, and particularly to Guillaume André, Martin Fougeras Lavergnolle, Razvan Ionica, and Anne-Marie De Matos.

The project represents a record of the work of all those who have encouraged and advised us. Though their names remain anonymous, I am greatly indebted to them; their involvement in the project is part of how we see architecture. Buildings and civil engineering projects stand as a concrete memory of our shared labors. Workers or engineers, these people are ready to meet the challenge; the project rests its hopes on their knowledge.

KOMA AMOK, our graphic designers, demonstrated a subtle finesse in their reproduction of the photographs illustrating the architecture of the projects. Aris Kafantaris has been invaluable in overseeing this publication.

Jean Attali played an essential part, both in listening to and clarifying our exchanges.

Acknowledgments of Erieta Attali

On July 14, 2016, I was fortunate to be invited by Farrokh Derakhshani, Director, Aga Khan Award for Architecture, to a conference at the Victoria and Albert Museum in London called Beyond the Bridge. In the list of speakers I saw the biography of a man named Marc Mimram. I didn't know him at the time, but I was curious to listen to him speaking about his bridges. Already before the end of his lecture, I realized that this had to be my next exploration in the world: I had to explore his infrastructure-scale works across France and beyond the borders of his country, his bridges, train stations, and swimming pools.
Up until Marc's lecture, I had already photographed monuments, both contemporary and historic, across the world. I had just completed my doctoral studies in Australia, with monographs on their way to being published. The timing felt right, then, for my visions and desires to be channeled to this new direction: a three-year journey over the works and sculptural creations of Marc Mimram.

I am thankful to Marc's trust, which was not to be taken for granted; instead, it was gained step by step, which gratefully led us to a moment of a great accomplishment: the completion of a circle of studies, decoding the landscape through infrastructure works spanning across landscapes, connecting and creating new realities for the life of all people.
It has also been a literal journey for me: coming from the most isolated edges of the world, where I spent over two decades, into the heart of Paris. And then, not only capturing Marc's works, but having the great opportunity to be sharing with him his visions and dreams.

Thank you Marc.

I am grateful to all the members of Marc Mimram Architecture et Ingénierie and especially to:
Anne-Marie De Matos, Marine Farouault, Cynthia Jupin,
Ignacio Olalquiaga Varela, et Liu Chengyin, China.

I am thankful to the following people for supporting several stages of this work:
Hatje Cantz, and specifically former managing director Holger Liebs, as well as Claire Cichy and all the Hatje Cantz staff, for having sincerely embraced my art and showing support throughout.
To all the translators and copy editors:
Aaron Bogart, Caroline Higgit, Anne Levine, Isabelle Liber.

Graphic design:
KOMA AMOK, Stuttgart-based graphic designers for their long-lasting devotion and the exceptional artistic intensity with which they dived into the complexity of this three-volume monograph, translating my photographic gaze and the ways with which I capture Marc's engineering and architecture, for their true faith and friendship.
Managing editor:
Aris Kafantaris, Tokyo-based architect, for his intellectual support throughout the process of this three-volume monograph on Marc Mimram; following every stage of the work from the birth of idea of this book to its completion.

Text contributors for the three monographs:
Jean Attali, Paul Chemetov, Sir Peter Cook, Ariel Genadt, and Zvi Hecker.

Photography services, and general assistance:
DIGID'A Lab in Rome. Davide Di Gianni and Fabio Barile,
with special thanks for the exceptional, high quality of their services.
Photography assistants:
Philipp Valente and Lukas Walcher, TUM University, Architecture;
Daniel Raphael Zuvia, Graduate School of Architecture,
Planning & Preservation, Columbia University, NYC.
Technical assistance for Roland-Garros Volume III:
Michel Ellert and Gilles Cargueray, Leica, France;
Charles Plumey, Paris.

And last but not least:
Lifelong respect to Kleio and Kazim.

Marc Mimram
Structure | Light · Landscapes of Gravity · Airtime
Through the Lens of Erieta Attali

Editor: Erieta Attali

Managing editor: Aris Kafantaris
Project management: Claire Cichy, Hatje Cantz
English copyediting: Aaron Bogart
French copyediting: Isabelle Liber
Translations: Anne Levine (French), Caroline Higgit (English)
Graphic design and concept:
Joerg Ewald Meißner, Gerd Sebastian Jakob,
KOMA AMOK, Kunstbüro für Gestaltung, Stuttgart
www.komaamok.com
Typeface: GT America (Noël Leu, with Seb McLauchlan)
Production: Heidrun Zimmermann, Hatje Cantz
Reproductions:
DIGID'A, Davide di Gianni, Fabio Barile, Rome, Italy
Jan Scheffler & Kerstin Wenzel GbR, Berlin
Paper: Condat matt Périgord, 170 g/m^2
Binding: Buchbinderei Terbeck GmbH, Coesfeld
Printing: Offsetdruckerei Karl Grammlich GmbH, Pliezhausen

Published by
Hatje Cantz Verlag GmbH
Mommsenstraße 27
10629 Berlin
www.hatjecantz.de
A Ganske Publishing Group Company

ISBN 978-3-7757-4403-4

Printed in Germany

Airtime

Developer: ICADE France
Owner: AG2R – La Mondiale
Steel company: Victor Buyck Steel Construction
Interior design architect associate: Leopold-Fauconnet Architectes
Situation: Avenue de France, 75013 Paris, France

MARC
MIMRAM
ARCHITECTURE
INGÉNIERIE

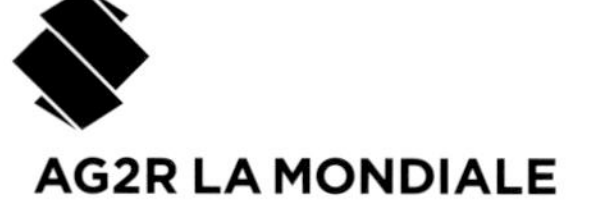